SECRET

HOUSTON

A GUIDE TO THE WEIRD, WONDERFUL, AND OBSCURE

William Dylan Powell

Library of Congress Control Number: 2019936697

ISBN: 9781681062099

Design by Jill Halpin

All photos provided by the author unless otherwise noted.

Printed in the United States of America
19 20 21 22 23   5 4 3 2 1

DEDICATION

To everyone still feeling the effects of Hurricane Harvey years later. CNN may have forgotten about you, but your neighbors have not.

CONTENTS

ACKNOWLEDGMENTS

Thanks to everyone who helped me look into Houston's weird, offbeat, and little-known phenomena. Special thanks to local historian, author, and archaeologist Louis Aulbach, whose impressive body of work and knowledge makes Houston a more interesting place. Thank you to the City of Houston and the Houston Police Department. Thanks to the people, businesses, and institutions who helped me to find facts and photos: Sam Houston Race Park, the Wilde Collection, the National Museum of Funeral History, Club Westside, the Orange Show Center for Visionary Art, Taste of Texas, George Ranch Historical Park, Inprint, Minneapple Pie, the Houston Livestock Show and Rodeo, Houston Dairymaids, Emerald Lake Resort, the Houston Museum of Natural Science, and Adrienne Saxe of Houston Greeters. Thanks to the kind Elizabeth Appleby at the San Jacinto Monument & Museum for her insights into the goings-on at the front line of Texas history (I let you guys off the hook, but I know how cool it is down there!). Thanks for those who took the time to brainstorm ideas for secrets, even when they were busy working on projects of their own—including Ken Fountain, Malcolm Wolter, and Donovan Buck. Much appreciation to the staff members at the Houston Metropolitan Research Center for their invaluable assistance. Thanks to helpful members of Reddit's r/Houston community, and to the fine gentlemen at University of Houston-Downtown and the Walter Prescott Webb Historical Society for responding to my queries. Fist bump to my wife Stephanie for serving as my part-time photo assistant, and to everyone in my Thursday night critique group for their patience. And an especially warm thank you to all the people who didn't tow my truck or call the cops on me when I was lurking around town taking all of these weird pictures.

INTRODUCTION

When a city reaches a certain age, a secret soon lives on every street. Sometimes that secret is a joy. Sometimes it's something else. But one thing is certain—with 6.9 million people in the Greater Houston area, we've got more than our share.

The crypt built into the banks of Buffalo Bayou. The ghosts of Patterson Road. The Palace of the Golden Orbs. I wrote *Secret Houston* to help bring some of H-Town's not-so-well-known places and past events to light. Many are things you can connect with and experience directly. Some are merely the shadows of long-forgotten legacies. But all are things you'd never know about, or wouldn't know to seek out, if you'd just stepped off an airplane to experience H-Town for the first time.

Some readers may know many of these already. Others may know none, but it's a rare few who'll be familiar with them all. To write this book, I consulted with historians, archivists, tour guides, community leaders, architects, archaeologists, business owners, other authors, and a number of local experts.

None of us will ever know all of Houston's secrets, and that's probably a good thing. But what I hope you get from this book is a little more enjoyment and appreciation of H-Town off the beaten path, with interesting reminders of the messy, interesting, and tragic, and maybe even a glimpse of the secrets that reside in your own neighborhood.

Share this book and then share your experiences on social media using #SecretHouston, and follow us on Twitter and Instagram (@SecretsofHTown). Because what's the fun of a good secret if you don't let others in on it?

KNOCK, KNOCK

Who's there? Casual Tex-Mex and live music behind a historic locked door.

Visitors to the Last Concert Café can expect the restaurant's distinctive red front door—which reads "Knock Twice & Cross the Border"—to be locked. Should someone let you in, you'll find a small restaurant and bar that serves hearty Tex-Mex favorites at reasonable prices, a pleasant outdoor courtyard, and a cozy stage out back that practically never cools down. In fact, at seventy years old, it's arguably the longest-running concert venue in town.

The Last Concert's locked door is more than just a gimmick. The original owners of what became the Last Concert Café in 1949 ran a house of ill repute. "Mama" Elena Lopez ran her original bordello from an old Victorian home just off Navigation Street. When the cops busted their main building, Lopez moved operations to another one of her family's properties—what is now the Last Concert Café.

Visitors will notice a small vertical window by the door; that's where management kept an eye out for cops. Guests had to knock before they came in—Lopez didn't want to get busted again. Once inside, customers could have a drink and relax. The inner courtyard was actually where the patrons would get to know the prostitutes via a "nickel dance."

The oldest part of the building—in the back (not open to the public these days)—was where the real business was conducted. In fact, bits of the original structure date back

Seventy years is a long time for a city of millions to keep a secret. But, given its legacy, Last Concert might just be the most secret-laden institution in H-Town.

LAST CONCERT CAFÉ

The original door of the Last Concert Café was kept closed because they had to keep an eye out for the law. These days, plenty of cops and lawyers come knocking, but only for the enchiladas.

WHAT Houston's hideaway for Tex-Mex and music

WHERE 1403 Nance St.

COST Lunches from $10–$20, shows start at free

PRO TIP Go on a nice day and enjoy the courtyard.

even farther. Parts of the buildings, going back to the plantation era, are from the 1840s. Some of the shiplap wood used in the restaurant's oldest construction could be, conservatively, about five hundred years old.

The owners declared "interruptus" on the prostitution gig in 1949, transitioning the place into the restaurant and concert hall we know today. Rumor has it that the freeway was supposed to cut right through the property, but the owners knew so many secrets about local politicians that it was rerouted.

2 BEAST MODE

What's the best place in town to watch camel races?

Texans have always loved the ancient sport of horse racing, and Sam Houston Race Park is H-Town's very own place to bet on the ponies. A real-life horse track, this place gives you the full traditional horse racing experience—parading thoroughbreds, trumpets blowing, dirt flying, screens to follow along, etc. Whether you're a lifetime fan or first-time visitor, they make it easy to have a fun day at the races. The track hosts events for the Kentucky Derby and Preakness Stakes, and it has more than five hundred televisions for simulcast betting (races taking place somewhere else).

But what many people don't know is that more than horses take to the track. You can also bet on races involving camels, zebras, adorable little corgis, and wiener dogs—and even ostriches. Yep, you read that right. Watch the schedule and you can cheer on a pack of thoroughbred wiener dogs as they run for high stakes. I mean, if you don't think watching a wiener dog wearing an adorable little number sprint for the finish line is fun, I'm not sure how to help you. They win every race by a nose. Corgis too are surprisingly fast, and all the dogs look so happy out there.

The ostriches have actual jockeys riding them, which must make for an interesting race from the rider's perspective.

The animals at the park are treated like royalty, with expert trainers and handlers. In fact, if you have a wiener dog or corgi—or camel, for that matter—you could be

---

Sam Houston Race Park isn't just about horses. You can also go watch camels, corgis, wiener dogs, and ostriches take to the field. The thing about ostrich races is that it's always neck-and-neck.

Camel races are just one of the interesting runs you'll find at Sam Houston Race Park. Camels actually have an interesting history in Texas. In 1856, the U.S. Army imported camels from around the world to Texas in an experiment called the "U.S. Camel Corps." The idea was that they'd be used as pack animals, but they were all sold off when the War between the States rolled around. Photo courtesy of Sam Houston Race Park.

SAM HOUSTON RACE PARK

WHAT Unexpected animal races

WHERE 7575 North Sam Houston Pkwy. W.

COST $8 adult admission during live racing

PRO TIP Watch the concert calendar, too.

the next celebrity race team. You may be on your own finding sponsors, though.

Bonus Secret: When there's not a race happening, Sam Houston Race Park is also an excellent concert venue, nailing down premium acts one after the other. Willie Nelson, Robert Earl Keen, Dwight Yoakam, Ray Wylie Hubbard, and the Josh Abbott Band have all played there.

And they're off!

³ SERIOUSLY WILDE SHOPPING

Where does a lover of the obscure go for the ultimate shopping trip?

The Wilde Collection is a shop in the Heights with an eclectic assortment of curiosities, taxidermy, avant-garde artwork, and conversation pieces. It struck the *Secret Houston* team as the kind of otherworldly shop that you might find a character stumbling into in an episode of the original *Twilight Zone* or Roald Dahl's *Tales of the Unexpected*.

The Wilde Collection is co-owned by Lawyer Douglas and Tyler Zottarelle, both passionate and discriminating art collectors. Lawyer is a big-time fan of Oscar Wilde; Tyler is into Edgar Allan Poe. So the two set out to create the kind of shop in which the ghosts of Wilde and Poe would feel at home. Although fulfilling this concept would surely require a well-stocked bar in the afterlife, our humble opinion is that they nailed the execution.

Calling the Wilde Collection a shop actually sells it short. You'll find unusual exhibits of the macabre, such as an old Odd Fellows lodge skeleton. There are a number of items with disturbing heritages, from an antique Ouija board with potential ties to the ghost of an axe murder to a terrifying Congolese demon vessel. The store sports tribal masks, statues, **Día de los Muertos** art, stuffed animals (and not the adorable kind), interesting furniture, some of the most

Part Oscar Wilde, part Edgar Allan Poe, part *Twilight Zone*—you have never been anywhere like this under-the-radar Heights boutique.

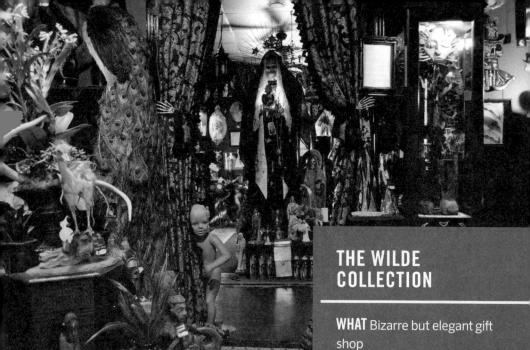

Just look at all of this awesome strangeness! Artwork, oddities, and antiquities come to the Wilde Collection from around the world. Photo courtesy of the Wilde Collection.

THE WILDE COLLECTION

WHAT Bizarre but elegant gift shop

WHERE 1446 Yale St.

COST Varies

PRO TIP Ask about the provenance of things you're interested in; the stories are a lot of the fun.

disturbing dolls ever, skulls, funereal accessories, odd jewelry, and strange, visionary bric-a-brac of all kinds. You'll also find multiple sets of eyes upon you as you browse—a result of the taxidermy on display.

The overall effect of the store is elegant, eerie, inspiring, and undeniably mysterious. We kept expecting to bump into David Sedaris perusing an antiquarian medical book or Stephen King asking about the provenance of a broken clock. We're planning on another trip there this weekend. So if you don't hear from us again, look in the back of the store for a shrunken, shaved head with glasses and a big, bushy beard.

<u>4</u> GOLDEN GLOBES

What's up with that giant golden globe over in Ashford Point?

If you're driving down the Westpark Tollway, you can't miss the Palace of the Golden Orbs—just west of Dairy Ashford between the tollway and Westpark Drive. The white, five-story building centered around a forty-foot Epcot-esque geodesic dome looks like something out of a Mayan-inspired sci-fi movie. You never see anyone there, and it's surrounded by a big parking lot and several undeveloped acres. All smack-dab in the middle of a working-class residential area.

Just what in the heck is this thing anyway?

The building is actually called the Chong Hua Sheng Mu Holy Palace, and it was built as a temple for a Hong Kong–based religious organization known as the Wu-Wei Tien Tao Association. Some sources report the group as Taoist; others describe a sort of Asian universalist religion. The group intended the building to be the centerpiece of a lifestyle center that was to include houses, retail shopping, childcare, and other conveniences to support their community.

Kwai Fun Yong, who was from Hong Kong, was leading the construction. But she was deported in 1999 and never came back. Apparently, she'd not gotten her immigration paperwork squared away, and was denied reentry into the United States. After this complication, the money for the project ran dry and the complex was never completed.

Sporting a forty-foot golden geodesic dome, this abandoned religious temple certainly promotes the philosophical value of letting go.

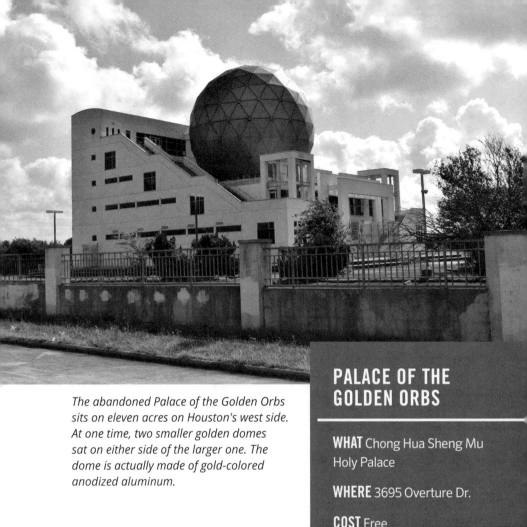

The abandoned Palace of the Golden Orbs sits on eleven acres on Houston's west side. At one time, two smaller golden domes sat on either side of the larger one. The dome is actually made of gold-colored anodized aluminum.

PALACE OF THE GOLDEN ORBS

WHAT Chong Hua Sheng Mu Holy Palace

WHERE 3695 Overture Dr.

COST Free

PRO TIP Stay outside the gates.

Houston's lack of zoning makes the complex a colorful addition to the Ashford Point area, with the surrounding undeveloped land emphasizing the building's big golden dome. The facility seems destined for the wrecking ball, although it looks to be in good shape and, I have to say, would make for a pretty cool office.

LIFE AND DEATH ON THE NORTHSIDE

What really happens when we die?

Behold the biggest secret of all. While death isn't a pleasant topic, curiosity about it is only natural. And that's what brings people to the National Museum of Funeral History, the nation's only museum dedicated to the rituals, artifacts, and industry surrounding the funereal experience.

You won't find corpses at the museum, but you will find a surprisingly fascinating and super-respectful experience that explores how we deal with death. The exhibits include funereal traditions of different cultures, a collection of cool old hearses (including the one that carried President Reagan), a history of cremation, a celebration of **Día de los Muertos,** an exhibit on nineteenth-century mourning rituals, an assortment of coffins and caskets, and more.

The museum was the brainchild of Robert L. Waltrip, founder of Service Corporation Inc., who turned his family-run funeral home into a public company with a market capitalization of more than $7 billion. Waltrip wanted to create a public place in which people could learn about the business of caring for the deceased.

It turns out that it's something people really want to know about. Today, the museum spans more than thirty thousand square feet with fifteen

---

NATIONAL MUSEUM OF FUNERAL HISTORY

WHAT Nation's only museum exploring rituals of passing

WHERE 415 Barren Springs Dr.

COST $10 Adults

PRO TIP The topic is scary and sad, but the place isn't. Give it a chance.

The museum's collection of vintage hearses. Funeral directors often refer to them as "funeral coaches" because it's a little less daunting. Photo courtesy of the National Museum of Funeral History.

permanent exhibits including the "Thanks for the Memories" celebrity memorial section, the history of embalming, and the Tomb of the Unknown Soldier exhibit. The museum collaborated with the Vatican on an exhibit called "Celebrating the Lives and Deaths of the Popes." You can even buy copies of famous people's death certificates.

Did you know that you can have a loved one made into a diamond? What's the difference between a coffin and a casket? In which country might you be buried in a coffin that looks like a tiger or a miniature Mercedes-Benz? Hit the National Museum of Funeral History for a viewing of all these secrets and more. But don't put it off, because, well, you never know.

"Death is not the opposite of life, but a part of it."
—Haruki Murakami

SECRET ASIAN LAND

Where can you find six thousand terra-cotta soldiers?

Lucky Land is a fun and heartfelt tribute to Chinese culture with the feel of an old-school roadside attraction, tucked unexpectedly among a series of northside flea markets and taquerias. A replica of Chinese emperor Qin Shi Huangdi's terra cotta army is the park's centerpiece.

Longtime Houstonians might remember these scale-model statues as the main attraction in Katy's Forbidden Gardens. Forbidden Gardens was the brainchild of a Hong Kong businessman who wanted to build a place where people could appreciate the wonders of Imperial China. It cost $20 million to build the huge theme park, which included not only the terra-cotta soldier replicas but also a number of scale model buildings and other exhibits.

Forbidden Gardens closed in 2011 when the state built the Grand Parkway.

The Lee family snapped up the army and a number of other pieces from Forbidden Gardens to build Lucky Land. They're an impressive sight: six thousand one-third-scale replicas of the emperor's soldiers, horses and all, complemented by scale models of ancient Chinese temples and more.

Lucky Land is a small, kitschy, family-owned theme park, and visitors can not only see the soldiers; they can roam the peaceful garden-like park and see awesome statues of Shaolin monks practicing kung fu, visit Panda Village, see the Happy Buddhas, and do other cool stuff. If you're especially lucky—and Chinese New Year is always

---

The original terra-cotta soldiers were buried with the self-proclaimed first emperor of China in 221 BC.

A number of statues adorn the park portraying various soldiers, tradesmen, and more. The kung fu warriors are awesome, but I found many of the more interesting ones to be people going about their everyday lives.

LUCKY LAND

WHAT Homegrown Asian theme park

WHERE 8629 Airline Dr.

COST $10 for adults

PRO TIP Sweep the leg.

great for this—you can catch special events including martial arts exhibitions, lion dances, and more. You can even take a rickshaw ride around the park! It's like being on the set of a Shaw Brothers film.

The sounds of the fountains, waterfalls, and traditional Chinese music create a relaxing vibe. Visitors are treated like royalty. For the *Secret Houston* team, the fact that you can hear Tejano music from next door only makes the place more endearing. We went twice.

LOGAN'S RUN

What's the hidden history of Memorial Park—one of the nation's largest urban greenspaces?

When Germany invaded Belgium in 1914, Americans considered it merely an interesting bit of news. But when it was revealed that Germany had proposed an alliance with Mexico that included the promise of regaining Texas and other lands, the United States assembled thirty military units almost overnight.

These soldiers needed training, and that's where Camp Logan came in. The "Memorial" in the Memorial Park name is a tribute to American World War I veterans, and this thriving urban park was once the site of an enormous National Guard training camp.

Named after a prominent Union officer who served during the War between the States, Camp Logan operated from 1917 until 1919. Although only around 3,000 acres were fully developed, the base stretched out across 9,500 acres around west Houston—with a rifle range between Gessner and the beltway, and an artillery range just west of Beltway 8.

Many of Camp Logan's soldiers-in-training lived in tents, although the camp also held more than 1,300 wooden buildings. It was like a city all its own with a post office, a YMCA, a library, mess halls, canteens, company stores, and more. It also had a base hospital and Red Cross facility.

Local archaeologists and historians have uncovered a number of subtle remains from Camp Logan within Memorial Park over the years, including the foundations of old buildings and equipment and the remnants of infrastructure.

MEMORIAL DAY *and* MEMORIAL PARK

Memorial Park was once the site of Camp Logan, a WWI U.S. Army training camp. The Hogg family purchased the former Camp Logan land after the war and then sold it to the City of Houston at cost with the intention of keeping it as a Park.

Memorial Park was named in dedication to the soldiers who lived and trained here. We are grateful on Memorial Day and every day for the ultimate sacrifice of soldiers who died in service of the United States of America.

On Memorial Day, the Memorial Park Conservancy, a group that does all kinds of good things for the park and those who enjoy it, puts flowers out in memory of those who fought and died in service of their country.

MEMORIAL PARK

WHAT Former WWI training camp

WHERE 6501 Memorial Dr.

COST Free

PRO TIP Stop by the Houston Arboretum and Nature Center at the western edge of the park and learn all about native Houston wildlife.

The base was hit hard by the influenza outbreak of 1918, losing more than eighty soldiers. It also served as the site of one of the nation's most horrific race riots, resulting in the largest ever U.S. court martial.

In 1924, the Houston City Council approved the purchase of approximately 1,500 acres of the former Camp Logan for use as a city park. The prominent Hogg family, who donated a significant portion of the land from their postwar holdings, named the park. While none of the buildings from the old Camp Logan remain, visitors can still find traces of the old military base, such as bits of foundation or road, if they look closely.

⁸ GHOSTS IN GRAY

If you stop along a bridge on Patterson Road, will Confederate ghosts actually touch your car? Or will you simply cause a horrific accident?

Legend has it that the ghosts of Confederate troops march down Patterson Road, between Highway 6 and North Eldridge Parkway in the Bear Creek area. Some say that if you turn off your lights and drive slowly or stop along the Langham Creek Bridge, you'll hear the undead troops tapping on your car as they march by. Others have claimed that the spectral soldiers have left fingerprints on their car or actually pushed them along. A few visitors have even reported actually seeing ghostly figures on the bridge.

Although there is no consensus as to its origin, rumor has it there was some sort of skirmish involving Confederate troops on that ground. Technically, the only major battle around Houston during the War between the States was in Galveston, but those were volatile times, and untold conflicts took place all over Texas.

It could have been a minor scrape between Union and Confederate troops, maybe long after Appomattox. Or maybe an instance of violence against anti-secessionist citizens. This seems possible, since Bear Creek was settled by Germans in the 1850s, and Germans across Texas were staunchly against secession. In fact, you can see the remains of the abandoned Hillendahl-Eggling Cemetery just north of Patterson Road, which once held original settlers. Many

---

Not only are ghosts reportedly seen walking Patterson Road, but the nearby abandoned cemetery is an interesting bit of local history. The cemetery was abandoned because of flooding in the area.

Legend says that the ghosts of Confederate troops march along Patterson Road and will tap on your car at the Langham Creek Bridge.

LANGHAM CREEK BRIDGE

WHAT Undead Confederate soldiers

WHERE Patterson Rd.

COST Free

PRO TIP Avoid hitchhikers eating hardtack.

call this abandoned graveyard the "Blue Light Cemetery," citing a ghostly light seen there at night.

Others say the tales have always been hogwash, or confusion over a battle having been fought at a different Bear Creek in another state.

Although it cuts through the woods, Patterson is a busy road. We can say with absolute certainty that something *will* happen if you stop your car on the Langham Creek Bridge and turn off all the lights. What will happen is that you'll cause a terrible, and possibly fatal, vehicular accident. Who knows—then maybe you'll be forced to haunt the bridge forever yourself. So if you check out this Houston secret, please do so safely.

SWAYZE'S SECRET SPOTS

These Houston haunts helped give the late, great Patrick Swayze the time of his life.

Native Houstonian Patrick Swayze was a Hollywood legend for his work in such films as *Red Dawn, The Outsiders, Dirty Dancing, Ghost, Donnie Darko,* and others. These are some of the places around town that had an impact on "Buddy," as he was then known, during his time in H-Town.

Patsy Swayze's Studio

Swayze's mother, Patricia "Patsy" Yvonne Helen (Karnes), began teaching Patrick to dance practically as soon as he was able to walk. Her studio was a major haunt for the *Ghost* star. The Houston Jazz Ballet was located at 3480 Ella Boulevard and 1355 Judiway Street—the current home of Move Yoga. Rumor has it that the Spot Club on 28th Street was also once the site of a Swayze studio (back where the pool tables are). Swayze's mother was also the dance choreographer for the film *Urban Cowboy*.

San Jacinto College

Sure, Swayze was a dancer. But the Waltrip High student was also that most prestigious and pure of Texas heroes, a high school football star. A knee injury put him out of the game, though, and dashed his college football scholarship dreams. San Jacinto College stepped up and gave him a gymnastics scholarship.

Houstonians of a certain age remember the late Patrick Swayze as a local boy who made it big. And if you know where to look, you can explore a number of his old haunts around town. Wolverines!

Swayze reportedly was a regular at Mytiburger in Oak Forest as a young man. He went by "Buddy" back in the day.

PATRICK SWAYZE'S H-TOWN

WHAT Swayze's secret spots

WHERE Oak Forest and then some

COST Free

PRO TIP Don't put Baby in the corner.

The Galleria Ice Rink

In 1971, Swayze took a job managing the ice-skating rink in the Galleria. Although he was still plagued by injuries, the gig led to a tour with Disney on Parade as, who else, Prince Charming in *Snow White*.

Gleannloch Farms

Patrick Swayze once visited this Arabian horse outfit, located in both Spring and Las Palmas, and acquired a passion for horses that lasted his entire life.

Mytiburger

The retro burger hangout Mytiburger at 2211 W. Forty-third Street would have seemed right at home on the set of the 1982 film *The Outsiders*. Swayze was a fan growing up.

<u>10</u> WHAT THE HECK IS A WARD?

You hear many neighborhoods around town referred to as "wards," so what's that all about?

A ward is an old-fashioned government district. The founders of Houston, the Allen brothers, hailed from New York. In the 1800s, parts of New York City were referred to as wards. Today's Garment District would be around Ward 20; Wall Street was in Ward 1. The Allen Brothers kept that structure for a number of Houston's original neighborhoods. Many older American cities, including Chicago, New Orleans, and Boston, originally used a ward structure.

The theory was that a mayor with centralized authority could wield too much power and weaken overall democratic representation. So if you split a city up into wards and elected an alderman to run each ward, the power would be shared. Aldermen held short terms and were elected frequently. Six wards were created in Houston's early years, four originally and two later on, each with their own political pulse and leadership. As Houston moved from the nineteenth to the twentieth century, it was having a number of growing pains, including—surprise!—drainage problems. In 1905, Houston voted to abolish the ward system in favor of a mayor-and-council structure.

Still, each "ward" remains an historic and distinctive part of Houston's past. The First Ward was the northwest bit of downtown at the time—from Commerce out to White Oak Bayou—and it has transformed from a commercial hub into the city's premier arts district. The Second Ward is to the southeast and became a hub of Mexican culture. The Third and Fourth Wards became support networks for the city's African American population. Fifth Ward in Northside

This sign stands outside Houston's Fifth Ward. If you're in the mood for a bit of local 1990s film, check out Greg Carter's film Fifth Ward. *It was also made into a 2018 television series. Carter has since moved to Los Angeles.*

became home to a number of industrial sites, and is now undergoing significant development. Many regard today's Sixth Ward to the west as outright gentrified. But each has had its struggles and triumphs over the years, and each holds its own secrets.

The concept behind Houston's original ward system was to decentralize power, as opposed to having a mayor's office that controls everything. Although this official political system is long gone, the monikers and history remain.

PARKWAY TO THE PAST

What was life like in Houston ten thousand years ago?

As part of the mandatory planning whenever a major freeway is built, the state sent a team of archaeological consultants to study the planned route of the Grand Parkway's Segment E, which runs between Interstate 10 and Highway 290. In 2012, this team found an extraordinary site of prehistoric significance along the banks of Cypress Creek where it intersects the Grand Parkway—a discovery that would provide a rare glimpse into Houston's prehistoric past.

Known as Dimond Knoll (that's actually the spelling), the site revealed human remains, tools, darts, pottery, bison teeth, spear tips, deer bones, hammerstones, and other antiquities dating back approximately ten thousand years. It was an exciting find for archaeologists, because relatively little is known about life in our area at that time. Recovered artifacts from the site dated from the Late Prehistoric to Middle and Late Archaic Periods, a remarkably broad period of time.

Life in the region ten thousand years ago for the oldest known peoples around Houston was very different—and we're not just talking about a lack of Starbucks. Paleo-Americans in the region hunted bison and deer, foraged for food, and fished to survive. To the east, the coastline actually looked different; the Texas Gulf Coast didn't settle into the shape we know today until between 3000 and 1000 BC.

Experts say that the old settlement might have been an early trading center, since a number of materials found are not indigenous to this part of the state. A number of pit-like features containing human remains were uncovered during the dig. Of course, the fact that it's a human burial ground warranted special consideration. The specific sites bearing

Plans for the Grand Parkway cut right through this ancient burial and trading site. The parkway goes over the area via bridge. The burial site is actually on the northern bank.

GRAND PARKWAY

WHAT Ancient burial site

WHERE Grand Parkway and Cypress Creek

COST Free

PRO TIP The specific burial site is difficult to access safely off the freeway. Maybe just appreciate this secret from afar.

native remains were left in peace covered in riprap and cement, and the road was suspended over the site via a bridge.

So—and this is especially fun to say around Halloween—today the Grand Parkway runs directly over an ancient Native American gravesite.

When they were building the Grand Parkway, workers recovered remains of prehistoric humans and other artifacts on the banks of Cypress Creek. It was a potentially wonderful discovery, since not much is known about life in the area more than ten thousand years ago.

GOING DOWN

Is Houston really sinking?

Yep, it sure is. The nation's fourth-largest city is flattening like a collapsed soufflé. In fact, the entire Houston and Galveston area is steadily sinking. A map by the U.S. Geological Survey on "Hydrogeology and Simulation of Groundwater Flow and Land-Surface Subsidence in the Northern Part of the Gulf Coast Aquifer System, Texas, 1891-2009" shows parts of town sinking at up to ten feet during that time.

Every Houstonian has a Hurricane Harvey story, but the storm certainly brought the issue to the forefront for many in town (especially those unaffected by previous flooding).

So what gives? Why are we losing ground? There are a number of reasons, and none of them are especially fun to think about.

For one thing, Houston is built on sand, clay, and gravel. In addition to causing foundation issues for a number of Houston homeowners, it turns out that this combination compacts quite a bit when you place a large metropolitan city on top of it. Unlike Austin, which is built on a combination of bedrock and the crushed dreams of tech entrepreneurs, Houston's soil cracks and shrinks with nothing to stop the squishing action.

Houston is sinking because of groundwater consumption, soil compaction, and other factors. In addition, the *Atlantic Monthly* reports that the 275 trillion pounds of water sitting on top of the city during Hurricane Harvey actually pushed the Earth's crust down by 2 centimeters. So we've got that going for us, too.

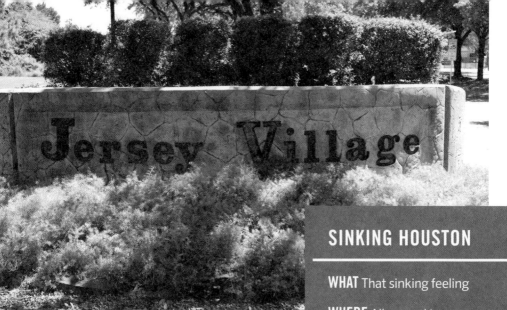

Some parts of town are sinking more quickly than others. Jersey Village, one recent report showed, is sinking about two inches per year.

SINKING HOUSTON

WHAT That sinking feeling

WHERE All around town

COST $125 billion for each Hurricane Harvey

PRO TIP Keep up with your flood insurance, bottled water, and church attendance.

The larger problem, however, is the management of underground aquifers.

Four million people and countless business enterprises take a lot of water to maintain—and we rely on underground springs to slake the city's thirst. But pumping water, and other things, out of the ground at scale can lower the surface elevation. It's sort of like when you let air out of a pool float—you're just that much closer to the wetness below.

Different parts of the city are sinking at different rates. In fact, the U.S. Geological Survey has created an online subsidence tool that lets you plug in a Houston address and see thirty-year elevation changes around various aquifers. Check it out at https://txpub.usgs.gov/houston_subsidence/home.

SECRET RENDEZVOUS

Where can Houstonians take their sweethearts for a little low-key quiet time?

Some call it a speakeasy. Some call it a make-out bar. But everyone agrees that this River Oaks icon is a hidden Houston treasure. If you'd never heard of it by word of mouth, it would be entirely possible to live near and pass by Marfreless and never know the place exists. There is no sign. They don't advertise much. From the outside, it's just an unremarkable gray door beneath a metal staircase. And yet, it has a reputation of being one of the most romantic little hideaways in Texas.

This sexy and stylish two-story lounge has a first floor that offers a cozy and well-appointed bar. Its dim mood lighting gives the bottles on offer, which are lit from the bottom, an ethereal glow. There are regulars as with any bar, and it's a great place to cool down from the Houston heat. The wine list is strong, and they know how to make your favorite drink.

But most people come for the upstairs.

The second floor of Marfreless offers a cozy arrangement of couches that lets you get snuggly and talk—or whatever—in relative privacy. With candles on the tables and discreet service that won't ruin the mood, this is a favorite for a late-night rendezvous or afternoon's sneaking

---

Visitors won't find the raw, bawdy Marfreless of yesteryear. Today's Marfreless is still hidden and discrete, but now a more upscale experience. If feelings of amorous bliss continue for more than four hours, consult your physician.

Behind this mysterious, unmarked gray door beneath a metal staircase off Peden and McDuffie Streets awaits an intimate lounge that's perfect for quiet cocktails for two (or more).

MARFRELESS

WHAT Cozy, hidden bar great for couples

WHERE 2006 Peden St.

COST Drinks + broken heart

PRO TIP Hit their sexy Halloween party.

away together. And for all that, the unmarked outside looks like the shipping entrance of a Michael's.

Today's Marfreless is sexy, respectable, and a tad upmarket. Nudity is not allowed, although it was back in the day when the place was under different ownership. Still, kissing passionately while stretched out on the couch upstairs is just another day at the office. And discretion is found in both the staff and clientele. So if you want to escape the rest of the world and spend some quiet time with that special someone, there's no better place in H-Town than Marfreless.

¹⁴ HIDDEN GEM

Is the key to a gemstone, buried by a deceased New York author, still somewhere in Hermann Park?

In 1981, Byron Preiss released a fantasy puzzle book called *The Secret*, featuring riddles and mystical illustrations that would lead readers to buried ceramic "casques" encased in plexiglass. Preiss had hidden these casques in twelve different cities. If you found one, he'd send you a $1,000 gemstone.

It was a cool concept, motivating readers to exercise their mind grapes and get outdoors. Across the pond, the publication of *Masquerade* by Kit Williams in 1979 had people tearing up garden allotments across England looking for a jewel-encrusted hare. So amateur treasure hunts were all the rage.

But in 2005, tragedy struck when Preiss was killed in a car wreck on New York's Montauk Highway.

At the time of his death, only two of the twelve casques he'd hidden had been found. In 1983, three clever teenagers found the Chicago casque buried in Grant Park. And in 2004, a bankruptcy attorney from New Jersey figured out the clue to the Cleveland casque and flew in just to dig it up. The ten remaining casques? For all anyone knows they remain hidden—including the one that Preiss hid in Houston.

The consensus by treasure hunters is that it's likely buried in Hermann Park near McGovern Lake, possibly beneath a walking trail. The park and its contents have changed a lot over the years, of course. If the Houston casque is where most people think it is, digging it up would be disruptive and difficult (and illegal). Keep in mind that Preiss didn't have any special permission to bury his casques. He simply went around with a shovel doing his thing.

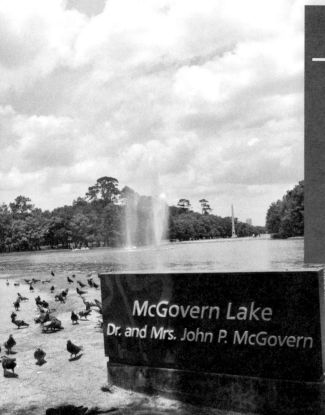

WHAT Clues to a puzzle from the past

WHERE Somewhere in Hermann Park

COST Free

PRO TIP For real, don't try digging it up.

McGovern Lake
Dr. and Mrs. John P. McGovern

The Hermann Park casque is said to be buried beneath a walking trail near McGovern Lake (not in this spot, so please don't dig here). The park once sported an old Southern Pacific steam engine that was part of the book's puzzle, but that train has since been relocated downtown.

For many, demystifying the clues would be reward enough. The author's widow, Sandi Mendelson, has taken up the mantle of awarding gemstones to those who present her with a key. But don't bother hitting up his family's survivors for clues. Preiss took those secrets with him.

Even after all these years, you'll still find furtive-looking treasure hunters out at Hermann Park marking off the spot where they think Preiss buried his casque and key.

¹⁵ SECRET SQUEEZE

Where can you find Houston's sweetest lemonade? Certainly not written down on a menu anywhere.

Tucked away on Chenevert near the ballpark, it would be easy to miss one of the most unique Mexican restaurants in town. Having lunch at Irma's Original is like eating at the home of a beloved aunt—a cozy space filled with knick-knacks, signed autographs, and H-Town memorabilia.

Everything about the food is a secret because there is no menu. They'll tell you what they have on any given day. And you'd better be courteous to your server, because the lack of a menu also means they'll charge what they please. People are happy to pay, because Houstonians love the place. It's a hotspot for downtown lawyers, bankers, oil executives, and the odd Houston Astros baseball player.

The James Beard Award–winning Irma Galvan started her eponymous restaurant in 1989, and over the years it's become a low-key Houston institution. She and her family take their work seriously and it shows. But nothing gets more buzz than the restaurant's lemonade.

Sweet, light, packed with ice, and filled with chunks of fruit, calling the lemonade at Irma's "lemonade" hardly does it justice. It's really more like a refreshing fruit punch. Efforts of the *Secret Houston* team to recreate the concoction at home have failed, but it's definitely got some combination of watermelon juice, lime juice, and lemon—along with huge

Served ice cold with generous chunks of seasonal fruit, Irma's lemonade is the perfect cure for a hot Houston summer. But don't bother asking for the recipe.

Irma's lemonade is a sweet secret you just have to know about in order to ask for. It actually has a lime base and enough fresh fruit to hydrate the most exhausted Astros fan after a game.

IRMA'S LEMONADE

WHAT The secret to surviving a Houston summer

WHERE Irma's Original, 22 N. Chenevert St.

COST Lap of the gods (no menus, no published prices)

PRO TIP Be on the lookout for Astros players.

chunks of fresh seasonal fruit such as pineapple, strawberry, and cantaloupe.

But what is the exact recipe for Irma's chunky, awesome lemonade?

We asked one of Irma's sons, Tony, as he worked the crowd during a recent lunch. Tony has the lean look of a weightlifting pro golfer, and as we chatted, he watched the door like a hawk—making sure everyone coming in found a table in the lunch crowd. When we mentioned the recipe, he took his eyes off the door and cocked an eyebrow as if trying to determine whether or not we were serious. "The recipe?" he said, shaking his head, "it's a secret."

SECRET CISTERN

Where can you find a cool, quiet, underground cavern in the middle of the city?

There's no better place for secrets than buried deep underground. And this subterranean secret under Buffalo Bayou Park was kept hidden for years.

A cistern catches water, usually rainwater, and stores it for future use. Back in the day, they were common in Texas homes; you still see them in rural areas or West Texas where water is scarce. While a well digs down to draw out groundwater, a cistern is just a big, water-tight bucket. In fact, the word *cistern* comes from the Latin *cista* for "box."

This particular cistern was built for the City of Houston in 1926 to help keep up with a surge in population. It had a capacity of 15 million gallons. An Olympic-size swimming pool, those huge 50-meter ones in which eight or ten people swim side-by-side, holds just over 660,253 gallons. So we're talking enough water to fill more than twenty Olympic pools. Or, converting it to popular Houstonian water measurements, it's the equivalent of almost 167 million glass bottles of Topo Chico.

The cistern served the city for more than eighty years. But in 2007, it was decommissioned because of a leak. There's not much use for a water container that won't hold water, so the space sat dormant for years. The Buffalo Bayou Partnership eventually restored and reinvented it as a public

---

For more than eighty years, what is now called the Buffalo Bayou Park Cistern provided Houstonians with clean drinking water. Now it's more of a creative wellspring.

The aboveground entrance to the cistern was added by Page Architects when the facility was repurposed as a public space. At one point, the City of Houston was looking for vendors to demolish it, but the Buffalo Bayou Partnership stepped in to save it.

BUFFALO BAYOU PARK CISTERN

WHAT 1920s water catchment turned art space

WHERE 105 Sabine St.

COST $5 for a thirty-minute guided tour

PRO TIP Make time to enjoy the rest of Buffalo Bayou Park while you're there.

space—adding a public entrance, walkways, lighting, and more.

This massive cavern is an impressive sight, cool and dark with more than two hundred twenty-five-foot columns that support the eight-inch-thick concrete roof. An echo lasts a solid seventeen seconds, and a shallow layer of water on the floor plays with the light. Not into dim underground spaces? An art installation called *Down Periscope* lets visitors to the park above look in it from ground level. And inside, various art installations and exhibitions make use of the cistern's lighting, space, and acoustics from time to time.

Cats loving climbing up high. So where are there four hidden cats higher than any other felines in town?

The Williams Tower is a 64-story Galleria-area icon that went up in 1983. Still known to many natives by its original name, the Transco Tower, the building was designed by John Burgee Architects with renowned architect Philip Johnson and in association with Morris Architects. Its revolving 7,000-watt beacon can't be missed at night. It's also the tallest building that's not downtown, and it's Houston's fourth-tallest building (the JPMorgan Chase Tower is the first).

Everyone knows that having an office in the Williams Tower makes a statement—with its enormous arched entryway, helipad, and nearby water wall and surrounding park. But what many Houstonians never notice is that the building has a secret: four hidden "cats" visible at the top of the tower.

The glass tower has a generally square shape as it rises to its full height, with a series of neo–art deco vertical lines running up the building. Like many art deco–inspired designs, these lines create a stepped, geometric outline. Near the top of the Williams Tower, you'll see that the corners of the building's square shape terminate in a narrowing fashion. And it's in these corners that you'll find the cats.

In each corner at the top of the building, you can clearly see the image of a sitting cat—a head with two ears, its

---

Did the building's designers work a hidden cat into the corners, or was it just a happy accident?

When you look at the top corners of the Williams Tower, you can see the image of a sitting cat, complete with head, ears, two front legs, and a tail that hangs down.

body, and two legs, along with a tail that runs down the corner of the building.

Is this an optical illusion or an intentional design feature? The urban legend surrounding these cats has is that architect Philip Johnson (1906–2005) loved cats and incorporated them into a number of his designs. The cats hiding in the corners of the Williams Tower resemble those classic Kit-Cat Klocks whose tails swing back and forth. But research into Johnson's alleged hidden cat designs seems thin. Were these catty corners an intentional Easter egg or just a happy accident? The truth remains fuzzy.

BANK VAULT

Where can you find a crypt from the 1860s tucked away in plain sight underneath a busy street?

When the Confederacy collapsed, Houston braced for the influx of Union soldiers. To keep munitions from falling into Northern hands, a number of these explosives were jettisoned into Buffalo Bayou. Stories abound regarding the contents of an arsenal being dumped by locals off the Milam Street Bridge, and of Confederate boats being piloted as far up Buffalo Bayou as possible and scuttled. It was better that these arms sleep with the catfish and alligator gar than wind up in the armories of your sworn enemy.

The problem was, of course, that these explosives and other discarded martial detritus stayed right where they were—piles of guns and cannonballs and shells and who knows what. Everyone in Houston knew the stuff was there, but Houstonians were busy picking up the pieces and getting on with their postwar lives.

On Sunday, February 10, 1867, twenty-two-year-old Henry Donnellan and his business partner reportedly took an unexploded shell from the bayou back to their shop, where they proceeded to hit it with a hammer. The results were not surprising. Working as advertised, the explosive blew the two men to bits.

Both men's modest remains were buried in the Donnellan family vault along the bayou. The crypt dates to 1849, and you can still see its entrance under the Franklin Street Bridge along Buffalo Bayou, just upstream from the Milam

---

Along the bank of the Buffalo Bayou under the Franklin Street Bridge, you can still see the entrance to a family crypt dating back to 1849.

The city has grown around the Donnellan family crypt for more than 165 years. The family's remains were removed when the Franklin Street Bridge was built above it. You can actually see the crypt from street level if you know where to look.

DONNELLAN FAMILY CRYPT

WHAT Mysterious gravesite from the 1800s

WHERE Beneath Franklin Street Bridge

COST Free

PRO TIP Get the whole story and more by taking the Buffalo Bayou Partnership's Looking Back History Tours (you can book tickets online).

Street Bridge. In the early 1900s, the Donnellans still in the crypt (four people total if you count Henry's friend) were relocated to Glenwood Cemetery. The city developed over and around the crypt, with the old bricks on the vault's arched entrance and wooden door still remaining.

In 1968, the "Southwestern Historical Exploration Society" recovered over one thousand War between the States articles buried in the bayou at the Milam Street Bridge. The Heritage Society eventually took possession of the items, none of which exploded. Do unrecovered Confederate explosives still await us beneath Buffalo Bayou? That's one Houston secret we hope is kept safe indefinitely.

¹⁹ BAYOU BUTTON

What happens when you press that mysterious unmarked red button at the Mosbacher Bridge? And who put it there?

The bridge passing over the bayou at Preston Street has a lot going on. Dedicated as the Mosbacher Bridge in 2016 by George H. W. and Barbara Bush, it serves as a memorial to heavy-hitting businessman, politician, and champion sailor Robert Mosbacher. The bridge sees a lot of foot traffic, being located between the Wortham Theater Center and Sesquicentennial Park, just across the bayou from the Downtown Aquarium.

So it's easy to miss the cheeky red button set to one side.

Built into a small nook in the southernmost corner of the bridge is an unmarked red button. No sign, no instructions, just a mysterious red button housed in the brick wall. Pressing the button will cause an enormous bubble to erupt from the bottom of the bayou. Locals call this "burping the bayou."

Officially called the *Big Bubble*, the button and subsequent murky burp is actually an art installation by artist Dean Ruck. Commissioned for the City of Houston by the Central Houston organization, the installation isn't just a bit of public fun. It also has an ecological role. When the bubble erupts, it helps to aerate the bayou—making the waters around the bridge less stagnant.

It's clever because wherever you have a red button just sitting out in the open, people are going to push it. And if

Pushing a mysterious red button tucked into a brick wall near the Mosbacher Bridge will cause a giant bubble to erupt in the middle of the bayou.

The button that engages the Big Bubble. *Hurricane season is not kind to the installation, so please have patience when it's down. It hasn't been very bubbly lately.*

PRESTON STREET BRIDGE

WHAT The *Big Bubble*

WHERE 510 Preston St.

COST Free

PRO TIP Check out the engraved metal towers above the button and all along the southeastern bank of the bayou.

nobody has the guts? The bubble will spontaneously erupt on its own, leaving passersby not in the know wondering what lies below. Local company Houston First Outdoors is charged with maintaining the mechanism, no mean feat given hundreds of curious fingers, bayou debris, and the occasional major hurricane. The installation has survived Tropical Storm Allison and Hurricanes Rita, Ike, and Harvey.

Originally called the Preston Avenue Bridge, back when Preston Street was Preston Avenue, the *Big Bubble*'s home was the first bridge crossing over the bayou. The original bridge on that spot was built in 1843, although the current bridge was built in 1914. The intricate artwork extending from the southeastern bank of the bayou from Prairie to Preston is part of a different installation by Mel Chin. These laser-etched metal columns are actually children's drawings made in 1986 representing Houston's seven great industries. The piece, called the *Seven Wonders*, was commissioned for the town's sesquicentennial and looks amazing at night.

CAJUN COMMUNION

Since when did a church cafeteria serve world-class Cajun cooking?

Christ Church Cathedral is Houston's oldest religious congregation, dating back to the Republic of Texas. Its current building was built in 1893, with some of the stained glass and other elements having been used in the previous structure. The church is one of the city's most cherished spiritual institutions, as well as one of its most in-demand wedding venues. Plus they make great red beans and rice.

The church's cloister—church talk for a sort of courtyard or plaza—contains a Cajun restaurant called Treebeards. This restaurant-in-a-cloister offers seating that's community style with long tables and plastic chairs. And the food is outstanding: red beans and rice with link sausage, shrimp etouffee, gumbo, jambalaya, homemade soups, salad, and more. Treebeards has a number of downtown locations, but this is the secret spot that's tucked discreetly away in a century-old church.

The restaurant at Christ Church Cathedral has always been known as The Cloister. Back when Treebeards had just its Market Square location, the owners approached the church and asked whether they could start handling its food service. And so they started dishing out heavenly home cooking at The Cloister in 1981. I can't attest to the food quality before the Treebeards takeover, but I've witnessed firsthand several of the entrees (and its butter pie) and can't imagine that it came close.

In addition to great food in a unique atmosphere, diners at The Cloister can experience The Cloister Gallery—an intimate art gallery featuring a diverse and interesting assortment of artists. This is a legitimate art space, rotating work regularly and serving as a nice accompaniment

"Abandon hope of dieting, all ye who enter here."

TREEBEARDS, THE CLOISTER

WHAT Gluttony

WHERE 1117 Texas Ave.

COST Entrée and two sides, $10.50–$12.50(ish)

PRO TIP Mustard greens help lower cholesterol.

to lunch. Recently featured artists have included Jan Golden, Ray Viator, Vicky Gooch, Mary Frankel, Keith J. R. Hollingsworth, Charlie Jean Sartwelle, and Rix Jennings.

So the next time you're downtown and looking for an out-of-the-way lunch, duck into Christ Church Cathedral for some of downtown's best home cooking. Grease be with you.

Meals at The Cloister in Christ Church Cathedral are served by Treebeards—a Zagat-rated restaurant offering hearty Cajun and home-cooked fare.

41

21

HOUSTON UNDERGROUND

Why don't you see crowds of office workers walking the streets of downtown Houston like in New York or Chicago?

Drive around the central downtown districts of most major cities and you'll see the streets packed with suit-wearing office workers crammed onto the sidewalk. But in Houston, where the high averages 91 degrees in July and August, tramping the blazing hot concrete in a suit jacket makes for some pretty miserable meetings.

That's why so many people who work downtown use the tunnels.

Houston's downtown tunnel system is a network of clean, air-conditioned tunnels that join ninety-five blocks of commercial, public, and residential space. Twenty feet underground, the tunnels are over six miles long and connect downtown buildings with restaurants, nail salons, optometrists, dry cleaners, gift shops, theaters and, of course, parking. All told, eighty buildings plug into the system. It's the largest tunnel network that does not contain a subway.

Houston's downtown tunnels got started in the 1930s as buildings were looking for ways to share infrastructure. In fact, one of the earliest tunnel developments began when an owner of movie houses connected multiple theaters underground for the purpose of sharing that most precious of Houston commodities, air conditioning.

If many people use the tunnels every day, though, how is this a secret? Well, most of the those familiar with the tunnels either work downtown or tramp through on their way from dinner to a show somewhere in the theater district. There are no obvious public entrances, and you have to go through a building like Wells Fargo Plaza to get in.

WELLS FARGO PLAZA

You can access the downtown tunnel system a number of ways, including through the Wells Fargo Plaza entrance at 1000 Louisiana Street.

DOWNTOWN TUNNEL SYSTEM

WHAT How downtown insiders stay cool

WHERE Downtown, Central Business District, Theater District

COST Free

PRO TIP Hit Tacos A Go Go while you're down there (on the tunnel loop), because they're not going to build a downtown tunnel system in Houston and not include tacos.

They're also closed evenings and weekends, so many people just don't have a reason to go down there.

But it's worth a trip. When the tunnels are open, you have a quick and comfortable way to get around downtown. No crossing dangerous streets, no black bus exhaust blowing in your face: just a healthy bit of exercise in a place that feels more like a mall than a tunnel system.

The downtown tunnels have grown organically over the years. So it doesn't feel as though it were all laid out according to a master plan (that's a very Houston thing). Color-coded maps help visitors get around, but if you really want to get to know the tunnels, you can take a guided tour.

Houston's downtown tunnel system gives Houstonians an air-conditioned and convenient way to get around without turning into a sweaty, disgusting mess in their nice work clothes.

22

FLIGHT TIMES

Where can you check into an airport from the past?

More than ten million people pass through Houston's William P. Hobby Airport each year. And most of them don't notice that tucked subtly inside the new airport, you'll find one of the most interesting secrets in Texas aviation: the old, original municipal airport.

A magnificently preserved example of art deco industrial architecture, the old 1940 airport terminal is located on the west side of the airport near Telephone Road. Between 1940 and 1955, the building served as the city's main airport. Today, the grand old terminal functions as the 1940 Air Terminal Museum, transporting visitors to a bygone era of passenger air travel when the experience still seemed glamorous and didn't yet resemble a miserable Third World gulag.

The old airport terminal would be worth a visit even without the museum's collection. Designed by architect Joseph Finger, who also designed city hall, it's a wonderful example of 1940s art deco with aviation-themed bas reliefs, marble floors, and a number of original touches (check out the cool old chandelier).

Its collection is wonderfully nostalgic, and it includes memorabilia from long-gone airlines such as Braniff and Texas International, model airplanes, articles, gauges, photos, tower controls, and all kinds of cool stuff. You'll see

---

Hidden alongside the modern William P. Hobby Airport lies the old Houston Municipal Airport terminal from the 1940s, a wonderfully restored art deco building now turned into a museum.

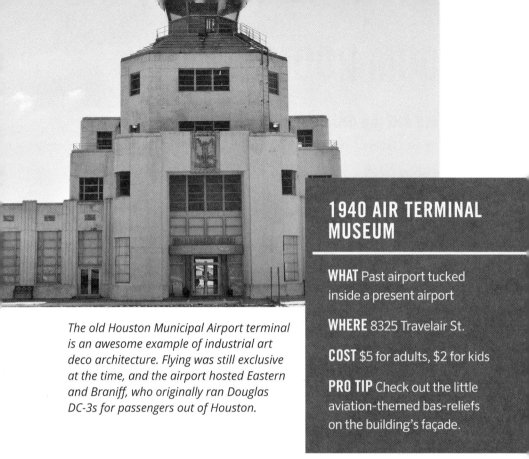

The old Houston Municipal Airport terminal is an awesome example of industrial art deco architecture. Flying was still exclusive at the time, and the airport hosted Eastern and Braniff, who originally ran Douglas DC-3s for passengers out of Houston.

1940 AIR TERMINAL MUSEUM

WHAT Past airport tucked inside a present airport

WHERE 8325 Travelair St.

COST $5 for adults, $2 for kids

PRO TIP Check out the little aviation-themed bas-reliefs on the building's façade.

the uniforms of old pilots and flight attendants—along with all of the pins, patches, and name tags.

The collection really does drive home how air travel has changed over the years. Case in point? Before overpriced Wi-Fi, playing cards were one way that passengers occupied their time during a flight. The museum has pack after pack of playing cards sporting Continental, United, and other airline logos. The museum also owns a number of vintage aircraft on display, including a Lockheed Model 18 Lodestar N31G and a cool old Sikorsky S-58 N887 helicopter from 1958.

People visit the 1940 Air Terminal Museum for different reasons today—some to attend events such as plane raffles or movie nights, others just to see the collection or building. But one of the most popular reasons is just to hang out and plane watch. People pass hours there simply watching airplanes come and go.

BOOM ROOMS

Where did the Allies keep bombs before air mailing them to Hitler? In part, the Ship Channel.

Not many people know about the now overgrown World War II–era bomb bunker just east of the bridge off the East Belt. This wasn't a bomb shelter, where people could be safe from a bomb blast. Just the opposite, in fact. The San Jacinto Ordinance Depot was the place you kept bombs before they went out into the world. To Hitler from Houston, with love.

Built between 1941 and 1942, the San Jacinto Ordinance Depot played a pivotal role in warfare logistics for the Allied forces. The facility's function was to receive, store, inspect, and repair bombs and ammunition as they came and went from the field. According to the Texas State Historical Association, the facility had shipped more than 208 million pounds of ammunition to the U.S. Army and U.S. Navy by 1945.

The remains sit on an almost five-thousand-acre patch of land south of Jacintoport Boulevard, west of the Stodlt Haven terminals. It was once part of a larger campus with multiple buildings to both store and destroy ammunition (which sounds pretty fun, actually), a wharf complex, and a railroad transfer station. When you look at the area on a map, you can see how perfect that spot would be—with rail lines on one side and the Ship Channel on the other.

The San Jacinto Ordinance Depot off Jacintoport was once a major distribution terminal for military ordinance. Now it looks like something from Indiana Jones, and it may or may not glow in the dark (kidding).

There is a 99.9% probability that a killer clown lives in each of these buildings.

SAN JACINTO ORDINANCE DEPOT

WHAT Abandoned WWII munitions facility

WHERE Jacintoport and the East Beltway

COST Free, except for tetanus and spider bites

PRO TIP Best appreciated from afar.

As World War II and Korea cooled off, there was less demand for actual ammo. In the 1960s, the government decided that we no longer needed the facility and sold it to the private sector for around $10 million. There's not much left today. The thick, sturdy buildings are overgrown with weeds and vines, and the whole facility is going through a remediation process.

You can still get in the buildings; its thick, metal doors are open, but it's not recommended. It's also private property. Because of its industrial nature, it's not a part of town you can just walk around safely, and getting hurt out there would be pretty easy. So appreciation from afar is probably your best bet.

24

IRISH GOODBYE

Can you spot the last remaining vestige of the once glorious Shamrock Hotel?

Back when the Texas Medical Center was still in its infancy, the area was home to the world-famous Shamrock Hotel: an eighteen-story resort built by eccentric oil tycoon Glenn H. McCarthy. And if you know where to look, you can still see the extravagant hotel's last remaining shadow.

Born in 1907, McCarthy was a Beaumont native and old-school wildcatter who struck it rich. Proud of his Irish heritage, McCarthy built the $21 million hotel as the first phase in a larger development that would grow alongside the medical center, and he spared no expense.

On St. Patrick's Day in 1949, 175 of the biggest Hollywood stars of the day—including Errol Flynn and Ginger Rogers—descended on the grand opening. Fifty thousand people attended the party, which cost $1 million (that's more than $10 million in today's dollars).

The Shamrock was the largest U.S. hotel built in the 1940s, with 1,100 rooms. Its swimming pool was the largest in the world, big enough to hold waterskiing exhibitions. Sixty-three different shades of green were used throughout the hotel. It had a popular nightclub and an exclusive private social club called the Cork Club. For a few years, ABC even produced a television show called Saturday at the Shamrock.

Approximately fifty thousand people showed up to the Shamrock Hotel's grand opening party on St. Patrick's Day 1949. Its pool was so huge that waterskiing exhibitions were held inside.

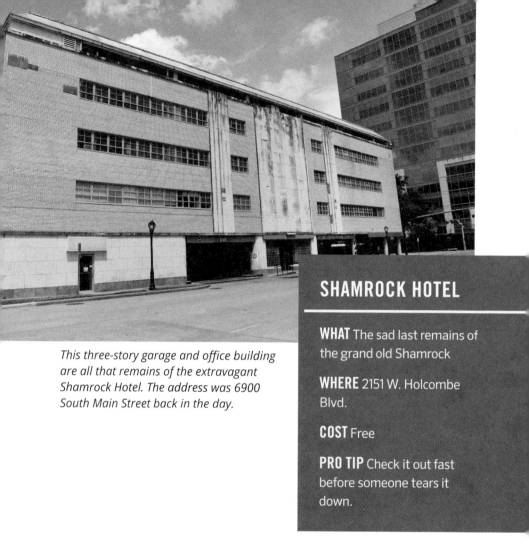

This three-story garage and office building are all that remains of the extravagant Shamrock Hotel. The address was 6900 South Main Street back in the day.

SHAMROCK HOTEL

WHAT The sad last remains of the grand old Shamrock

WHERE 2151 W. Holcombe Blvd.

COST Free

PRO TIP Check it out fast before someone tears it down.

McCarthy and his hotel were fictionalized in the movie *Giant*, staring James Dean, Rock Hudson, and Elizabeth Taylor.

All this glamor didn't come cheap. The Shamrock needed 82 percent occupancy just to break even. Soon McCarthy couldn't keep up the expense. By the mid-1950s, it had become the Shamrock Hilton. On St. Patrick's Day in 1986, its luck ran out for good and the building was razed.

But you can still see its old parking garage at 2151 W. Holcombe—the Shamrock's last surviving structure. The first floor serves as parking for the Texas Medical Center (Garage 8), with an upstairs housing the med center campus of University of Houston–Clear Lake.

25

SPRING TRAINING

Do you know about Minute Maid Park's hidden past?

With its grand archways, fluted columns, and marble floors, Minute Maid Park's visitors get the feeling they're experiencing something historic (in addition to watching the World Series Champion Houston Astros baseball team). And that's because the lobby of the ballpark has a hidden past: it was once one of the busiest train stations in town.

If you look at the west end of the stadium, you can see the distinctive red brick lobby at Texas and Crawford that was once the terminal of Union Station. Built in 1911 by the same architects who designed Grand Central Station in New York, Union Station cost $5 million to build. An elegant construction at the time, with high ceilings and three different types of marble, it would ride out the golden era of rail travel in Houston.

Houston was a major rail hub in this part of the country back in the day. It even earned the moniker "Where seventeen railroads meet the sea." Union Station connected the Burlington Northern, Santa Fe, and Missouri Pacific lines. Over the years, millions of travelers came and went through Union Station dressed in dapper travel clothes, eating at the station's cafes, and waving tearful goodbyes. After World War II, rail travel began tapering off. Trains stopped running through the facility in 1974.

Today it's the cornerstone of Minute Maid Park. You can see where the stadium's architects drew inspiration from the old terminal's original Classical Revival architecture. Completed in 2000, renovating the station into the entrance of a ballpark with over forty thousand seats cost $250 million. The backers of the project included Enron's Ken Lay, hence the stadium's original name: Enron Field.

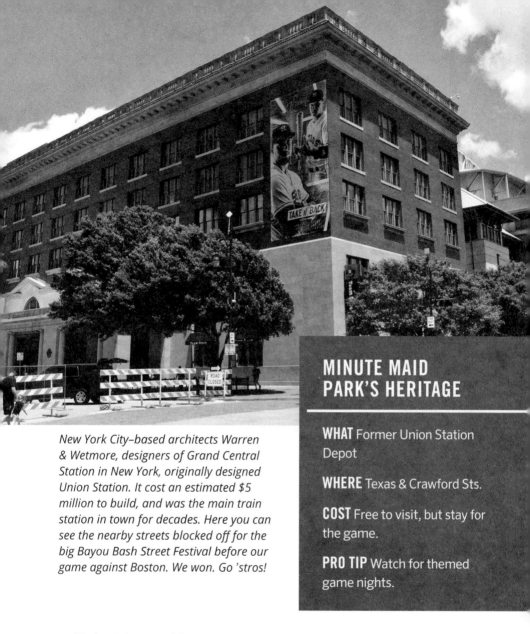

New York City–based architects Warren & Wetmore, designers of Grand Central Station in New York, originally designed Union Station. It cost an estimated $5 million to build, and was the main train station in town for decades. Here you can see the nearby streets blocked off for the big Bayou Bash Street Festival before our game against Boston. We won. Go 'stros!

MINUTE MAID PARK'S HERITAGE

WHAT Former Union Station Depot

WHERE Texas & Crawford Sts.

COST Free to visit, but stay for the game.

PRO TIP Watch for themed game nights.

Today it's possible to visit a game at the ballpark and miss the building's past as a major rail hub. That's why the park's larger-than-life replica train is on hand to help celebrate all those 'stros home runs.

The lobby of Minute Maid Park had a former life as Union Station, the largest rail terminal in the Southwest.

26

ALL TAPPED OUT

Want to raise a glass to a once great brewing empire?

Saint Arnold. Karbach. Buffalo Bayou Brewing Company. Modern Houston is by no means short on breweries. But back in the day, the beers getting the most buzz around town were all made at the Houston Ice & Brewing Company's Magnolia Brewery.

In 1915, the Magnolia Brewery spanned twenty acres on both sides of Buffalo Bayou downtown. The complex had ten buildings, including a huge five-story main complex with towering smokestacks and offices at Milam and Franklin. It made hundreds of thousands of barrels of beer per year, with brands that included Southern Select (its most popular), Extra Pale, Standard, and Richelieu.

The place had an absolute wizard of a brew master—a Belgian named Frantz Brogniez. Under his direction, the brewery's Southern Select beer even won the Grand Prize at the International Congress of Brewers in 1913. So why have so few people heard of Magnolia Brewery? Prohibition.

Trying to work around the federal government, the owners retooled the place in 1918 as the Magnolia Dairy Products Company, making butter, ice cream, milk, cottage cheese, and more. But business was flat. Harvey-like floods destroyed various buildings along the way. And by the time Prohibition was repealed in 1933, there was no saving it. Oil magnate Howard Hughes started the Gulf Brewing Company in 1933, hiring Brogniez and rebranding the old

The Magnolia Brewery was once a twenty-acre facility on both sides of the bayou, cranking out some of Houston's favorite beer before Prohibition.

The brewery's old office building was designed by H. C. Cooke and Co. in 1912. As of this writing, the old offices were abandoned—just one of many businesses still disrupted after Hurricane Harvey.

MAGNOLIA BREWERY

WHAT All that's left of a once great brewing empire

WHERE 717 Franklin St.

COST Free

PRO TIP This is right by the Donnellan crypt, so you can see them both at once.

Southern Select recipe under the name Grand Prize beer. But Gulf Brewing, too, went under.

Today all that's left of the old Magnolia Brewery is its former office building at Milam and Franklin—until recently a British-style pub called the Brewery Tap. The building has since been sold. Hurricane Harvey hit it hard, and as of this writing the building was abandoned (though permits were posted). I have faith that the building will come back to life. Although many people might not have heard of the old Magnolia Brewery, everyone knows there's nothing like a cold beer in the Houston heat.

27

OASIS OUT WEST

Where can West Houston residents serve and be served amidst toucans and tigers?

Despite its 16.5 acres, it's very possible to drive by Club Westside daily and never know it's there. The only clue visible from the road is its racket-shaped sign—the rest is tucked away. But missing it would be a shame, though, because it offers a much-needed respite for stressed-out Houstonians.

Originally the Westside Tennis Club, this massive facility served as a major tennis destination. It had almost fifty courts sporting a variety of surfaces from grass to red clay. At various times, Westside hosted the ATP U.S. Men's Clay Court Championships. All the greats played there.

But in 2007, owner and CEO Linda McIngvale had a vision. She wanted Westside to be more than just a tennis mecca, and she spent $10 million transforming Westside Tennis Club into an urban oasis known today as Club Westside.

The place still has a ton of courts and the tennis instruction and competition you'd expect in a quality tennis club. But now it also has a 15,000-square-foot fitness center, an incredible yoga studio, pilates, boot camps, an indoor running track, a virtual cycling studio, weights, a ton of cardio equipment, and personal trainers.

Sound too intense? There are beaucoup swimming pools, including a 32-person jacuzzi and a multi-million-dollar lazy river. There's a sports lounge, a café, steam rooms, massages, and more. This secret hideaway is super kid-friendly, too, with a complimentary arcade, bowling, climbing, and other fun stuff for kids. Plus, there's complimentary childcare so you can hand off the kiddo and take a quick swim.

This adorable little thing is just one of many animals that reside on-site at the club. Photo courtesy of Club Westside.

CLUB WESTSIDE

WHAT Low-profile club where the family can recharge

WHERE 1200 Wilcrest Dr.

COST Varies by membership type

PRO TIP Tap into a yoga class.

And did we mention the exotic animals? You can't have an oasis without wildlife. The lineup changes, but members get to hang out with exotic birds, capuchin monkeys, baby giraffes, tiger cubs, a huge tortoise named Tank, and other favorites. It's like a country club, only without the stuffiness—and with monkeys. So if you're on the west side and feel yourself starting to stress, join the club.

Once just a tennis club, today's Club Westside is a hidden westside gem with something to help everyone in the family de-stress.

28

LOST AND FOUND

Do you know the hidden history behind the bell and clock in the tower at Market Square?

Back in the day, early Houstonians came together at the big City Hall and Market House downtown. There people could do their banking or get their mail, and maybe settle a dispute at the City Hall. They could also knock out a bit of shopping—buying fresh produce farmer's market style. It was a great place for all the latest gossip in a world before social media.

Houston had four similar City Hall and Market House buildings over the years, and each had a fire bell and huge clock tower. The third burned down, but its 2,800-pound bell, cast in 1876 in Pittsburgh, was saved. When the fourth was built in 1904, it used the old bell and had a Seth Thomas clock with a face that measured seven-and-a-half feet across.

As the city grew and Houstonians became more mobile, the facility saw less and less use. In 1939, Houston's current art deco–style City Hall at 901 Bagby was completed. Eventually the old City Hall and Market House complex became a bus station and the building was demolished, its clock stored in a crate.

Fast forward to the 1980s. Someone ran across a really cool looking bell in an East Texas junkyard. He purchased

---

Both the clock and the bell in the Market Square Clock Tower had secret lives doing service in the old City Hall and Market Square building that was demolished in the 1960s. The clock was found in a crate, and the bell was discovered at an historical park in Woodville, Texas, in 1988.

The old Market Square Clock Tower at Travis and Congress Streets. That's Hotel ICON in the background, originally built as the Union National Bank in 1911. It was one of the city's first concrete and steel skyscrapers.

MARKET SQUARE CLOCK TOWER

WHAT Once forgotten clock and bell with an historic heritage

WHERE 301 Travis St.

COST Free

PRO TIP Get a picture taken at the "Houston Is Inspired" mural next door at Travis and Preston.

it and put it on display in a public park in Woodville, Texas. Eventually, someone in Houston figured out the bell's significance and bought it—bringing it back home to the Bayou City.

Today the old clock and bell both live in what is known as the Market Square Clock Tower (a.k.a. the Louis and Annie Friedman Clock Tower). The clock needs winding every eight days. In 2013, Houston artist Ann Fleischhauer augmented the clock with a cool art installation that would add a variety of interesting artwork to the clock's faces. Good to have you back, big guys.

29

WHAT FRIES BENEATH

Where can Houstonians eat a juicy buffalo burger beneath the freeway?

Directly beneath the Westpark Tollway, just outside the Loop, lies one of the best burger joints in town. Bubba's Texas Burger Shack has been serving up delicious burgers for thirty years—way before the freeway came along. This quaint, family-owned place truly is a humble little shack, with a wide front porch always packed with diners and a hand-painted sign out front reading "Icehouse." Founded by Bubba Gilliam, the building used to be a key shop on Westheimer before it became a burger place and was moved to its current location. In 1990, one of the restaurant's regulars, Richard K. Reed, bought it.

Bubba's will put its beef burgers up against any in town, but it's really known as the home of the buffalo burger. Bubba's has bison meat brought in from South Dakota, and they do amazing things with it. Leaner than turkey, it's seasoned and cooked deliciously, yet has less fat and cholesterol than conventional beef. Bison also don't require a bunch of hormones or antibiotics, so it's a cleaner burger.

They've served over a million buffalo burgers, and the construction of the Westpark didn't slow them down. Bubba's doesn't have many neighbors. When they built the freeway, practically every business around moved or closed because of construction. But despite having to hop a curb and drive through a construction site, people just kept coming to Bubba's. They like to joke that they offer "covered parking" now that the Westpark looms overhead.

You may have to speak up a little on the porch because of the road noise, but truly nobody cares. The burgers are great, the beer is cold, and the afternoon crowd looks way happier than those sitting in traffic. They have a food truck

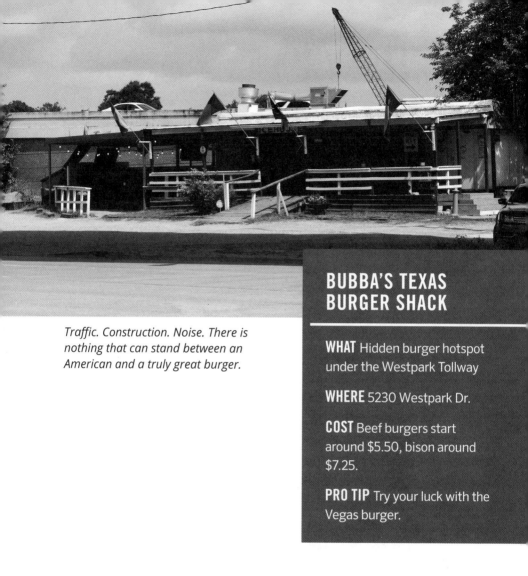

Traffic. Construction. Noise. There is nothing that can stand between an American and a truly great burger.

BUBBA'S TEXAS BURGER SHACK

WHAT Hidden burger hotspot under the Westpark Tollway

WHERE 5230 Westpark Dr.

COST Beef burgers start around $5.50, bison around $7.25.

PRO TIP Try your luck with the Vegas burger.

that takes buffalo burgers on the road, and they'll even sell you bison patties, steaks, and other cuts—along with their own secret habanero sauce and Es Bueno secret seasoning. Es bueno, indeed.

Tucked under the Westpark Tollway, Bubba's is a hidden hotspot famous for its bison burgers and buckets of cold beer.

How do Houstonians make an island escape on the cheap?

Island decor. Exotica music. Fruity drinks. Lei Low is a good old-fashioned tiki bar, replete with thatched bar accoutrements, little umbrellas for your drinks, lots of island flair, and a smattering of souvenir parrots. And it's truly a secret hideaway. Lei Low is tucked away onto the end of a Heights convenience store. The only sign visible from the street reads: "Stop at Joe's Food Store." Pull into the far left of the store and you'll see your first clue that the place even exists: a modest Polynesian-style wall mural.

Once you discover this island treasure, though, you're in for a piece of kitsch paradise. A friendly neighborhood bar, Lei Low treats visitors like VIP tourists. Dark and cool like the cave Tom Hanks lived in on *Cast Away*, the mellow vibe hits you right away. Whatever you were worrying about out in the world floats away like a coconut shell in the current. There's a back patio, regular exotica concerts and live music, a "Lei Low Land Lovers Rum Club," and lots of fun little things that keep your lounge experience interesting.

The word *tiki* is a Maori word referring to the first men in Polynesian mythology—typically represented by a sculpture or carving. The phenomenon of the Tiki bar is attributed to a bootlegger named Ernest Raymond Beaumont Gantt,

LEI LOW RUM & TIKI BAR

WHAT Hidden tiki hideaway with exotic flavor

WHERE 6412 N. Main St.

COST Drinks start around $7.

PRO TIP Watch the bartenders work; they're amazing.

You will drive right by this place unless you look for the canoe out front, next to the "Stop at Joe's Food Store." I'm convinced people buy homes in the neighborhood just so they can walk to this bar when cocktail hour rolls around.

who went by the name Donn Beach. After traveling the South Pacific, he opened a Los Angeles bar in 1934 called "Don the Beachcomber." Its popularity kicked off a craze of island-themed escapes, and Lei Low is now carrying the tiki torch in his tradition.

Legend has it that if you steal glassware from Lei Low, you'll be cursed by the island gods, like in that episode of the Brady Bunch where Bobby took the tiki statue from Hawaii. So leave it where you drank it, unless you want to wake up with a tarantula in your bed.

Lei Low is Houston's ultimate tiki bar, with an incredible rum selection and a lei'd back atmosphere like no other place in H-Town.

31

ACT II, NEW SCENE

Do you know the story behind the columns that make up the Mecom-Rockwell Colonnade Fountain?

As the nation's largest free-of-charge outdoor performance hall, there's nothing secret about Miller Outdoor Theatre. The current facility was built in 1968 and looks like something out of a sci-fi movie. With an air-conditioned stage, a $1.5 million sound system and a packed schedule of award-winning performances, it's a popular spot for a picnic and free show.

But many Houstonians don't know that the Miller actually predates its current building.

The old, original Miller Outdoor Theatre was built way back in 1923. Its namesake was Jesse Wright Miller, a wealthy cotton broker and mining engineer who donated the land. Designed by William Ward Watkin, who designed buildings at both Rice University and Texas Tech, the old Miller had a classical Greek proscenium–style stage flanked by twenty Doric columns.

The opening performance of the old Miller was an extravagant production called "Springtime of Our Nation" and involved more than two thousand performers! That's a heck of a catering tab. But in 1968, voters approved a bond to build the fancy new theater you know today. If you know where to look, though, you can still see a part of the original Greek proscenium–style Miller building.

These columns in Hermann Park had a secret life before being a part of this colonnade and fountain— the original Doric columns in the first iteration of Miller Outdoor Theatre.

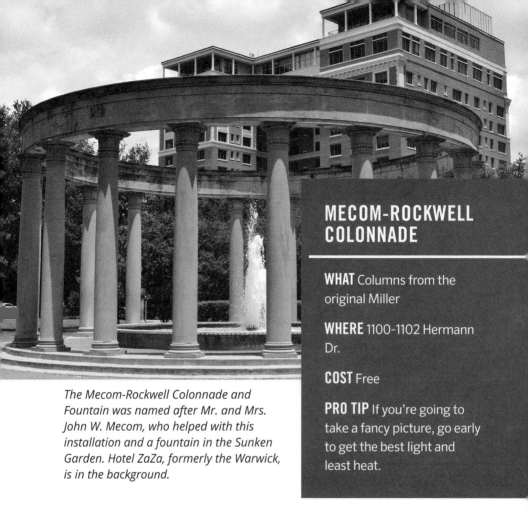

MECOM-ROCKWELL COLONNADE

WHAT Columns from the original Miller

WHERE 1100-1102 Hermann Dr.

COST Free

PRO TIP If you're going to take a fancy picture, go early to get the best light and least heat.

The Mecom-Rockwell Colonnade and Fountain was named after Mr. and Mrs. John W. Mecom, who helped with this installation and a fountain in the Sunken Garden. Hotel ZaZa, formerly the Warwick, is in the background.

When the city built the new Miller, it saved the twenty Doric columns from its original structure. The columns were then used to make the Mecom-Rockwell Colonnade and Fountain. Right in front of the tony Warwick Towers building in Hermann Park, the original columns—going on one hundred years old now—form the colonnade encircling the fountain. On any given weekend, you'll find all kinds of Houstonians hanging around, having wedding or quinceañera photos taken or just enjoying the peaceful sounds.

If those old columns could talk, they might tell some fascinating stories about past performances or surly gossip about Houston's theater community—or maybe just keep belting out "I am the very model of a modern major-general . . ."

32

LOCK 'N' LOVE

Where can you find Houston's answer to the Paris lock bridge?

The "lock bridge" trend started in Paris somewhere around 2008 on the Pont Neuf, Paris's oldest standing bridge, and other bridges in the area. It goes like this: lovers write their names or initials on a padlock and clamp the lock on the fence over the bridge. Then they toss the key into the water, symbolizing their everlasting love. Awww.

The idea really caught on in Paris—maybe a little too much. In 2015, Paris officials had to cut down the locks along the Pont des Artes bridge because collectively they weighed forty-five tons! That's twenty Ford F150 pickup trucks. All those little locks actually threatened the bridge's structural integrity.

Houston actually has two lock bridges. The first and most popular is the Rosemont Bridge that goes over both Memorial Drive and Buffalo Bayou. One bridge east of the Waugh Bat Colony, it's a romantic spot with a beautiful view of downtown. It doesn't much look like the lock bridges in Paris, though, since the sides aren't chain link. Houston is a city of engineers. The railings along the Rosemont Bridge are made of thick iron bars that look as though they'd survive a bomb. So couples attach locks to the thinner supports beneath the bars.

Houston's lock bridges are H-Town's version of the lock bridge in Paris. When Paris officials cut down sections of the Pont des Artes bridge in 2015, it had more than seven hundred thousand locks attached. That's a lot of love.

A ménage a trois, presumably.

LOCK IN YOUR LOVE

WHAT Lock Bridge

WHERE Rosemont Pedestrian Bridge

COST Free

PRO TIP Bougie couples get their locks engraved.

The second is a small pedestrian bridge that goes over Allen Parkway, just east of Eleanor Tinsley Park. The chain link sides more closely resemble its Parisian inspiration, but you're above Allen Parkway. Toss a key below and you could wind up in Huntsville with an altogether different love life.

Some people think the locks look trashy or that it's dangerous. And unless you lock up in one of these two spots, the city will likely cut it off in an effort to not have every Houston bridge groaning with five-dollar padlocks. But it's a quaint tradition many have latched onto over the years. *Vivent les mariés!*

33

DOMESTIC BEER

How did a home in Rice Military come to be covered in thirty thousand beer cans?

Rice Military has been a hot real estate area for years. Work your way into the neighborhood to Malone Street, and you'll discover one old home that's cooled off quite a bit over the years—with the help of about thirty thousand cold ones.

John Martin Milkovisch was an upholsterer for the Southern Pacific railroad. A hardworking guy, he enjoyed a cold beer at the end of a long day at work. He'd listen to classical music or opera and sit out front drinking an ice-cold Dixie, Falstaff, or Buckhorn beer—whatever was on sale, really.

In the late 1960s, Milkovisch began adorning his home with decorative flourishes—small at first. A fence with marbles that would catch the light just right. Custom cement pavers. Then it became more ambitious: concrete siding that featured found materials, a mounted tricone drill bit left behind from a Schlumberger job. Then, when he retired, he began decorating the house with beer cans he'd been saving for the previous seventeen years.

Needing a hands-on project in his retirement, Milkovisch spent almost two decades covering and decorating his home with beer cans: flattened cans comprising a makeshift aluminum siding, garlands made from can tops and bottoms, chains made from pull-tabs, decorations from peeled labels, flat-can ceiling tiles, and more. At first, he earned a few quizzical looks, but somewhere along the way the project reached critical mass and became a beloved conversation piece. Today it's world-famous as a kitschy art installation.

The Beer Can House is a part of the Orange Show Center for Visionary Art—encouraging free self-expression through

The front door of the Beer Can House. Milkovisch's wife actually scattered his ashes at the house after his death in 1988, so it is both his life's work and his memorial.

BEER CAN HOUSE

WHAT Kitschy home-turned-art-installation featuring 30,000 cans

WHERE 222 Malone St.

COST $5

PRO TIP Hours and days change depending on the time of year, so check out https://www.orangeshow.org for details.

a number of projects and programs around town. All kinds of philanthropic organizations have supported its restoration, maintenance, and operation. And if you come at the right time, you can get a docent-led tour. So tap in when you get a chance.

John Milkovisch began decorating his house in beer cans and other found materials in 1968; today it's one of Houston's kitschiest art experiences.

34

CONCRETE JUNGLE

Have you seen the monument to safety and wisdom on the East Side?

If you don't look closely, there's not much to see at EaDo's Freund and North Hutcheson. The old street marker is overgrown, as are much of the streets. But dig around in the brush on the corner and you'll notice a large, ornately carved marker that stands as the last remaining relic of an old industrial facility. The marker proclaims "Safety Follows Wisdom" and features two allegorical figures representing each of these virtues, the classical design of the sculpture giving visitors the feel of an archaeologist discovering a long-lost city.

This marker was one of several erected around the country by the Portland Cement Association to commemorate plants with a perfect safety record. It was presented to the Houston location of the Trinity Portland Cement Company, now just an empty slab, in 1929. The inscription reads:

> Portland Cement Association
> Safety Trophy Award
> Trinity Portland Cement Company
> Houston Texas Plant for a
> Perfect Safety Record in 1929
>
> Rewarded for a Perfect Safety Record in
> 1945, 1947, 1959

The facility was one of three Trinity Portland plants in Texas. It made a special high-temp cement for oilfield projects and was an important materials supplier during World War II. The plant closed in 1976, and only this sculpture now remains. Its design was the result of a contest held in the early 1920s, won by a group of students at the

SAFETY FOLLO

Hidden in the overgrown weeds at Freund and North Hutcheson on the East Side, this monument was awarded to a long-gone cement factory. The factory made a special high-temp cement that was good for oil and gas applications.

LOST CEMENT FACTORY

WHAT Forgotten industrial monument

WHERE Freund and North Hutcheson Sts.

COST Free

PRO TIP Stay safe yourself and watch your step in the weeds.

Art Institute of Chicago studying under Czech-American sculptor Albin Polasek.

One of the most popular construction materials in the world, concrete is used in greater quantities than water. Portland Cement (named after the British Isle of Portland) is the basic ingredient comprising concrete. It's basically a combination of calcium, silicon, iron, and other materials heated at high temperature and then finely ground before being mixed with sand and rock. In 2018, the United States made around eighty-five million tons of masonry cement.

Fun fact: Between 2011 and 2013, China used more cement than the United States used in the entire twentieth century.

35

BACKWARDS BAR

?noitarbelec tsol-gnol a rof deman rab ykriuq a dnif snainotsuoH nac erehW

Retro video games. Hockey. Kung fu. High-end art. Giant Kool-Aid men. In a city of four million people, there is no shortage of quirky dive bars. But there's nothing quirkier than Main Street's Notsuoh.

Notsuoh (Houston spelled backwards) is the King of Quirk on the Houston bar scene. Notsuoh has a low-key vibe with oddball throwback décor, cheap drinks, chess games, and a main stage featuring live music, art performances, comedy, and poetry. By design, the place draws all kinds of people, and you're as likely to bump into an oil and gas executive as you are an artist, hipster, or student.

But it's not just the funkiness or the speakeasy vibe, or even the giant misleading sign that reads "Clarks" out front, that earns Notsuoh a spot in *Secret Houston*. It's also the secret behind the name.

From 1899 to 1915, Notsuoh was the biggest party in town. In fact, the whole city shut down for this weeklong festival that served as Houston's answer to Mardi Gras. Massive street parades with intricate floats clogged the streets. People wore elaborate costumes, and many basically just drank all week. There was also a lot of college football, with UT and A&M playing games during the festival—as well as Rice and LSU.

New Orleans and Houston were commercial rivals at the time. Houston business owners wanted to use the party

This quirky downtown bar is named after a long-forgotten celebration that was once all the rage in Houston.

Notsuoh has a storefront, but it's tucked away inside the old Clark's building.

NOTSUOH

WHAT Quirky bar whose name has a secret past

WHERE 314 Main St.

COST Free + cost of drinks

PRO TIP Watch the event calendar and go when there's something particularly interesting on tap.

as a way to tout Houston's agricultural and industrial might. During the Notsuoh festival, everything was spelled backwards. The festival declared royalty such as King Nottoc for the cotton industry, Retaw for the port, Lio for oil, etc.

The old Notsuoh party ended when World War I rolled around, and the tradition was never brought back to life. But the people at Notsuoh on modern day Main Street are still ready to have a good time if you are. gniht siht od s'tel oS.

How many model ships have you ever seen in one place?

Jim Manzolillo loved boats. He carved his first boat at the age of six, served as a Merchant Marine during World War II, owned a shipyard in Mexico, and worked at the prestigious Cunard Line. His passion for ships, combined with a lifetime of extensive travel, meant that he'd collected an astonishing amount of maritime memorabilia. We're talking more than one hundred model ships, maps, sextants—all kinds of seagoing treasures. In fact, when I interviewed him for an article in *Texas Highways* years ago, he even showed me some stuff Neil Armstrong had brought to the moon (apparently the two used to sail together).

Eventually, Manzolillo reached out to the Houston Museum of Natural Science and generously offered to donate this amazing collection to the museum. They never called him back. So he decided to start his own museum: The Houston Maritime Museum.

The goal of the museum is to celebrate maritime history, marine industry, and the region's maritime legacy. Manzolillo passed away in 2007, but his vision lives on in a thriving institution that's become one of Houston's best kept museum secrets.

Visitors to the museum can see exhibits showcasing old-time sailing ships straight from a Patrick O'Brian story, steam-powered boats from back in the day, the vessels of the merchant marines, modern warships, ships from the War between the States, and more. There are model ships in a bottle (how do they do that?), authentic period navigation instruments, and, of course, exhibits on offshore oil and gas.

Guest lecturers are always popping in to give interesting talks and presentations. Recent topics have included the

Set Sail with

HOUSTON MARITIME MUSEUM

The Houston Maritime Museum is actually a great place for a party or meeting. Want to motivate your sales team? Tell 'em you want those numbers up ASAP or they'll be keelhauled.

HOUSTON MARITIME MUSEUM

WHAT Model ships crammed stem-to-stern

WHERE 2311 Canal St.

COST Adults $8

PRO TIP Try lunch at Andes Café, the South American joint next door.

1949 Texas City Disaster, an actual pilot's take on navigating the Houston Ship Channel, rainwater conservation, and how to eat and drink like a sailor (no word on cussing). It also hosts the Gulf Coast Ship Model Society. Permission to come aboard granted.

Where else but Canal Street would you celebrate Houston's maritime heritage?

37 CHEAP ROUNDS UNDERGROUND

Is there really a super-cheap bar hidden on the Rice University campus?

Sometimes referred to as the Harvard of the South, Rice University is consistently ranked as one of the nation's top schools. Fewer than 10 percent of all applicants are accepted, and the world's most brilliant minds have been drawn to its lush campus for more than one hundred years. And if there's anything students appreciate after a long day's thesis wrangling, it's cheap beer. Enter Valhalla.

Designed to be more elusive than a research grant, Valhalla is actually in the basement of Rice University's Keck Hall. Built in 1925 as the school's original chemistry building, it houses the study of bioengineering, molecular biophysics, biochemistry, cell biology, and a bunch of other brainy disciplines. The bar's entrance is a large wooden door on the backside of the stairs leading into the building—though the patio seating outside gives it away, especially on a nice day.

More than forty years old, Valhalla was originally meant to be a place where grad students could kick back with a cold one on campus. Today, the bar's cheap drinks and intellectual repartee draw people outside the university scene to the bar, though it's still mostly an owl's nest. The bartenders are actually unpaid volunteers with some association to the school.

Valhalla has been a graduate student pub on campus for more than forty years. In Norse mythology, Valhalla is the "hall of the fallen," where the god Odin receives heroes who've died honorably in battle.

This shady little spot under a staircase in Rice University's Keck Hall houses the underground bar that's as renowned for its intellectual conversation as it is for its cheap beer.

VALHALLA

WHAT Cheap basement bar on the Rice University campus

WHERE 6100 Main St.

COST Beer starts around $1.

PRO TIP Don't wear a necktie, and bring cash.

Valhalla is a cozy, casual space. It has a select few beers on tap, and dozens of bottled beers from a cooler. So if you can't find a beer you like, you're just being difficult. I paid less than a buck for my beer. It's cash only, and don't forget the part about bartenders being volunteers, so tip well. Also, you'll notice neckties hung on the wall like trophy game. This is not an idle threat; you've been warned.

Rumors of Rice students and alumni intentionally giving the bar one-star reviews online to discourage patronage by the unwashed masses from beyond the hedges have not been confirmed.

38

ROOM 322

Can you really ask for a secret underground suite at the Hotel ZaZa?

A few years ago, the Internet was abuzz about a strange room at the Hotel ZaZa in Houston's Museum District. Built in 1926 (originally the Warwick Hotel), it has a reputation for over-the-top glitz and eccentricity. Every room in the Hotel ZaZa seems decadent, and its fancy "Magnificent Seven" rooms are absolutely extravagant.

But among the most interesting are its themed concept suites. The "Houston We Have a Problem" room is decked out with NASA collectibles and space-themed furniture. Geisha House, Casa Blanca—each provide a unique experience, and you can find them all on the hotel website. All except for one.

There is a secret suite at Houston's Museum District Hotel ZaZa that's not advertised—you have to ask for it. And it's had conspiracy theorists running rampant with speculation. The room's concept? Prison.

A fraction of the size of other rooms at the hotel, the Hard Times suite is decorated with exposed brick walls, a concrete floor, and a bed that's chained to the wall. There is an embedded mirror reminiscent of a police interrogation room above the bed and an oversized painting of a skull on one wall. The framed photograph of a former Stanford Group executive stares at you from above the television.

The Hard Times room is a concept suite that you won't find on the Hotel ZaZa's website—a tiny, secret hidden suite with a prison theme. The room service is much better than Huntsville.

The Hotel Zaza in the Museum District has a number of concept suites that include Geisha House, Casa Blanca, An Affair to Remember, Houston We Have a Problem, and Soho Loft. But you won't find Room 322 on the list.

HOTEL ZAZA

WHAT Mysterious shadow suite

WHERE 5701 Main St.

COST Call for pricing.

PRO TIP Book ahead of time.

When rumors of the secret room first went viral in 2013, the hotel's spokesperson painted the room as simply a creative way to use an undersized space, but many still find something mysterious about it. Why isn't it advertised publicly like the other suites? What's the connection with the hotel and the Stanford exec? Is there really a secret "Skull and Bones" society connection to the number 322? Is there some *Eyes Wide Shut* stuff going on here?

Nobody knows for sure. But if you ever find yourself in a spot of legal bother, and have to do a little time, one could do worse than the ZaZa.

39

SECRET SPECIALS

Like ordering off the beaten path? Try these off-menu items.

Taste of Texas Secret Tower Cake

Taste of Texas isn't just a steakhouse; it's a Houston institution. And it offers a special dessert that's not on the restaurant's dessert tray—because it won't fit. The Texas Tower Chocolate Cake has four layers and stands seven inches tall, requiring structural support with a few chocolate straws. They also have a cinnamon coffee that's not only complimentary but also not on the menu. Don't forget to hit the in-house butcher shop.

Flamin' Hot Secret at Bernie's

If you're a fan of the good old-fashioned burgers found at Bernie's Burger Bus, ask for this messy, beautiful, sort-of-angry secret unicorn burger: The Flamin' Hot Cheetos Burger. Get this: the "buns" are made from mac and cheese encrusted with Flamin' Hot Cheetos; it comes with two meat patties, cheese, pecan-smoked bacon, a homemade "fire sauce," and crispy Tabasco onions. God, I love this country.

Chuy's Classified Appetizer

You won't find it on the Chuy's Tex Mex menu, but regulars in the know hit their server up for the Chuy Gooey Dip. As if their salsa fresca and creamy jalapeño ranch weren't enough, this secret snack is a layered dip made with refried beans, ground sirloin, guacamole, queso, pico, jalapeños, and lettuce.

Torchy's Tacos Secret Menu

Taco allegiances can be a sensitive thing in Houston. But if you're on Team Torchy's, you're in luck because they have a whole "secret menu." The *Secret Houston* team tried them

The Texas Tower Chocolate Cake is so tall that it needs chocolate straws to remain upright. All the chocolate straws in the world wouldn't keep me upright after eating that thing, but I'm sure willing to try. Photo courtesy of Taste of Texas.

OFF THE EATEN PATH

WHAT Off menu dishes

WHERE All over town

COST $3.95–$40

PRO TIP. Ask the server at your favorite restaurant what's off menu and they might just surprise you.

all but one, and can personally recommend both the "Trailer Park Hillbilly Style" with fried chicken and the "Ace of Spades" with sausage, brisket, fried egg, and more.

Lamb Lollipop at the Lodge

The Rainbow Lodge is one of my favorite places in town to get wild game. Also enticing is their secret rosemary and garlic-roasted Lollipop Lamb Chop appetizer. Rumor has it they also do an off-menu buffalo chili when the weather turns cool.

Sometimes when something is removed from the menu, a restaurant can and will still make it for you—for a time, anyway.

Ever wish you could visit a 1980s arcade, but still drink today's beer?

At an easy-to-miss corner of downtown near Minute Maid Park, there lies a portal to another time. A place that's never heard of Steam, Angry Birds, or PlayStation. A place where the power pellets flow like New Coke and having the High Score still means everything. A place called Joystix Classic Games & Pinballs.

Joystix is not a bar most of the time. It's actually a place where you can buy or rent all kinds of arcade games from modern to retro to sports. The place is packed with them, from old-school Pac-Man, Donkey Kong, and Dragon's Lair to Golden Tee golf. The place has been in business since 1987, when some of these games were still in their heyday. Today they're in amazing condition, even the old ones. Some of the old pinball machines are real works of retro pop art.

JOYSTIX

WHAT Pac-Man Fever Fridays at Joystix

WHERE 1820 Franklin St.

COST $15 per person, unlimited play

PRO TIP This isn't an arcade; it's a store. So unless it's Pac-Man Fever Friday, you have to make an appointment to visit and see all of these awesome games. It fills up quickly, so go early.

On the first and last Fridays of the month, the place transforms from showroom to game room—opening up for something they call "Pac-Man Fever Fridays."

During Pac-Man Fever, Joystix becomes a surprisingly hot nightspot. You get unlimited play at all the machines for just fifteen bucks. And this is strictly a grown-up affair—lasting from 9:00 p.m. until 2:00 a.m., with drinks available at the

Joystix challenges passersby to forgo the world of Oculus, high-powered consoles, and networked multiplayer games for the simple pleasure of eating a Pac-Man power pellet. Flock of Seagulls haircut not included.

Eighteen Twenty Lounge next door. The Lounge can hook you up with ice cold 8th Wonder and Saint Arnolds craft beer, mixed drinks, and more while you make it to the next level and earn those extra lives.

When it's Pac-Man Fever Friday, Joystix and the Eighteen Twenty Lounge come together to bring you pure gaming joy more powerful than the bliss of firing with two Galaga ships at once. They even crank up the '80s tunes to give the place an authentic retro feel a la *Stranger Things*. And its location makes it a perfect place for Friday Astros or Dynamo games. Insert coin now.

For two Fridays a month, the video game rental masters at Joystix throw open the doors for a late-night, booze-fueled, '80s-music-packed happy hour known as Pac-Man Fever Fridays.

41 SECRETS OF OLD TEXAS

Have you ever driven thirty minutes and gone back in time?

It's easy to live in modern-day Houston and forget about its frontier past. Most people don't know what life was like back in the day, before cars and freeways, before air conditioning or COSTCO or fancy coffee—even before Texas was a state. Fortunately, the George Ranch Historical Park is here to help fill you in on the secrets of yesterday's Texas.

George Ranch is actually a twenty-two-thousand-acre working Texas ranch and historical park. About thirty miles southwest of downtown Houston, it lets you explore life in old time Texas as it unfolds before you. The park actually has a clever design. It's set up around four different homesteads—each representing a different generation of a single family. These separate areas include the 1830s Jones Stock Farm, the 1860s Ryon Prairie Home, the 1890s Davis Victorian Complex, and the 1930s George Cattle Complex. Visitors get a sense of how Texas changed for regular families over the years.

The land that makes up the ranch was actually land from one of Stephen F. Austin's "Old Three Hundred" families, who originally helped settle Texas as a Mexican colony.

Period actors populate the museum bit of the ranch, working cattle and churning butter like it's just another day at the office. How are horseshoes made? What's a day in the life for an actual cowboy? There was no Whataburger, so what did people eat back then? The docents and actors reveal all these secrets and more as you go from exhibit to exhibit.

Rustic and as Texas-flavored as Dublin Dr Pepper, George Ranch has actually become one of the most fashionable wedding venues around town. If you really want a treat, plan

The self-sufficient lifestyle of a rancher back in the day meant collectively knowing how to do everything from make bread to breed livestock. Photo courtesy of George Ranch Historical Park.

GEORGE RANCH HISTORICAL PARK

WHAT Recreation of old time Texas

WHERE 10215 FM 762 Rd., Richmond, TX 77469

COST $15 for adults

PRO TIP Visit for the holidays; they really do it up around Christmastime.

your visit around Christmastime. They deck out Mamie and Albert George's old 1930s house for the holidays, complete with accoutrements by their dear friend Gene Autry—who actually wrote *Rudolph the Red-Nosed Reindeer*.

George Ranch Historical Park lets you step back in time and explore how life was lived back in old Texas across several generations. The George family held more than twenty thousand acres.

⁴² UNDERGROUND INFORMATION

Who was Louis Kung, and what did he build in Montgomery?

The northside town of Montgomery has a big secret—a forty-thousand-square-foot secret. And its story begins on the other side of the world.

Shanghai-born Ling-Chieh "Louis" Kung was the nephew of former Chinese leader Chiang Kai-Shek. His mother's family was enormously wealthy, and his father was the Chinese finance minister. He grew up to become a diplomat, eventually founding an oil company and moving to Texas with his wife, a Hollywood starlet. It was a rough life. But no matter what your circumstances, all men have fears. And, like many during the Cold War, Kung feared World War III.

A prepper before it was cool, in the early 1980s Kung upgraded the company's corporate campus in Montgomery with what looked like pleasant Asian pagodas next to a one-acre manmade lake. But like some paranoid-but-genius Bond villain, Kung had built, not a park, but the bulletproof secret entrance to an $18 million underground bomb shelter.

Just south of Highway 105, his complex was actually below the manmade lake—the water engineered to serve as a neutron barrier. A closer look at those pagodas revealed armor plating and gun turrets. Below, past the four-foot walls and blast-proof doors, Kung built a shelter designed to protect hundreds of people for months. The facility included decontamination showers, dorms, backup power, water wells, an intensive care unit, separate restrooms for men and women, conjugal visit rooms, and even a jail. The structure was built to survive a twenty-megaton blast as close as four miles away.

Hurricanes. Power quality issues. External data security threats. No matter what kind of crazy goes on in the outside world, Westland Bunker clients are able to continue business as usual.

THE WESTLAND BUNKER

WHAT Elaborate underground bunker built by nephew of Chiang Kai-Shek

WHERE 550 Club Dr., Montgomery, TX 77316

COST Priceless when needed

PRO TIP Due to the nature of their business, this secret facility is not open to the public. Also, get in good with these guys before the zombie apocalypse.

Kung went bust in 1988 and lost the property, dying in 1996. But his bunker lives on. In fact, today it serves as one of the world's most secure data centers. The Westland Bunker is a Tier III data center that provides governments, Fortune 500 companies, and other enterprises a strategically secure colocation, business continuity, and disaster recovery resource. Kung would be proud.

An eccentric Chinese businessman built this elaborate underground bunker in the early 1980s, which today serves as one of the world's most secure data centers.

BEER CAN HOUSE (page 66)

SMITHER PARK (page 104)

CLUB WESTSIDE (page 54)

ECLECTIC MENAGERIE PARK (page 160)

ART CAR MUSEUM (page 196)

DESTINATION MOUND TOWN (page 148)

LUCKY LAND (page 12)

ROOFTOP CINEMA CLUB (page 186)

GEORGE RANCH (page 82)

HERMANN PARK (page 28)

LOCK BRIDGE (page 64)

THE ORANGE SHOW (page 126)

SAM HOUSTON RACE PARK (page 4)

MOUNT RUSH HOUR (page 142)

BEDAZZLED

What does it look like when three hundred artists mosaic an entire public space?

Just off the Gulf Freeway near the University of Houston you'll find a small, half-acre park covered in folk art. Beautiful and chaotic all at once, Smither Park is a long green strip in a low-key neighborhood that sparkles in the sunshine with eclectic art made from bits of broken glass, pottery, tile, and other found materials—all lovingly crafted by talented creatives.

If you're not looking for it, the stunning assemblage of swings, arches, tiles, furniture, murals, and other interesting installations all connected by a mosaic walkway takes you by surprise. A big, patchwork amphitheater resembling a giant fish mouth stands at one end of the park—complete with sparkling disco ball hanging high above. On a lucky night, you'll catch some free music. There's a cool marble-roll tower, an intricately decorated pavilion, a memory wall, a mediation garden, and a lovely Día de los Muertos–style couple sitting at an outdoor table.

All this is tucked away in a modest neighborhood behind what looks like a junkyard for old shipping pallets.

Smither Park's namesakes are the late John H. and Stephanie Smither, who were big-time supporters of folk art here in town. It's a project sponsored by the prominent arts group the Orange Show, whose showcase property is next

---

Smither Park is a creative urban park space made and maintained by community artists—and loved by everyone. Lead designer Dan Phillips was the mastermind behind the park's design.

Even the tables are interesting at Smither Park, making it an excellent spot for a summer picnic. There's also the occasional show at the park's Lindley Fish Amphitheater.

SMITHER PARK

WHAT Volunteer-run residential art space

WHERE 2441 Munger St.

COST Free

PRO TIP Hit the Orange Show next door.

to the park. The purpose of the project is to promote self-taught art. And you can be part of this outdoor gallery, too, with no prior experience. Just reach out to the Orange Show and they'll let you know how you can get involved.

Every surface of the park is mesmerizing: the flowering memory wall with its giant butterfly, the throne-and-crown installation, hidden faces, crazy creatures, angels, antlers, tigers, landscapes, guitars, and who knows what else. And the beauty of this secret spot is that every time you go, something different is happening—from workshops and performances to weddings and parties. See? Art doesn't have to be stuffy after all.

44

THE TREE BRANCHES OF GOVERNMENT

Is there really an old oak from which Houstonians once hung criminals?

At the intersection of Capitol and Bagby stands a wizened old oak tree, where legend has it that lawmen of yesteryear carried out the harshest of criminal sentences. In fact, a plaque under the tree states that at least eleven criminals were hanged from the Old Hanging Oak during the Republic of Texas years (1836–1845). Frontier Texas was filled with such legends, with every town between the Red River and the Rio Grande purporting to have such a tree.

How accurate are legends of the Old Hanging Oak? The *Secret Houston* team contacted local historian Louis Aulbach for his opinion on whether the tree was actually a notorious executioner's tree.

Aulbach says, "The large oak tree near the corner of Capitol Avenue and Bagby Street, now known as the 'Old Hanging Oak' because of the sign placed near it, was part of the landscaping for the home of prominent Houstonian J. H. S. Stanley and his family. Stanley immigrated to Houston in the early 1840s, and the family lived on the property until the early 1880s. The county purchased the property in 1895 for a new county jail and courthouse.

"Although there were executions (by hanging) in Houston from 1837 until the 1890s, those executions were held

This old oak tree in front of Bayou Place has a hundred-plus-year history as a notorious part of the criminal justice system in early Houston. But its bark is worse than its bite.

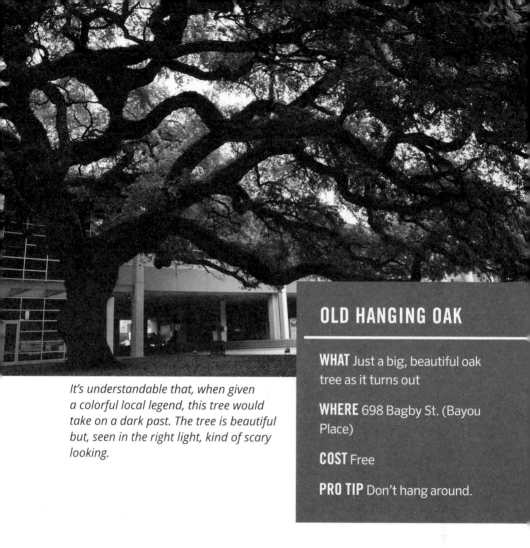

It's understandable that, when given a colorful local legend, this tree would take on a dark past. The tree is beautiful but, seen in the right light, kind of scary looking.

OLD HANGING OAK

WHAT Just a big, beautiful oak tree as it turns out

WHERE 698 Bagby St. (Bayou Place)

COST Free

PRO TIP Don't hang around.

at the prior locations of the county jail. It is not possible that executions took place at the so-called Old Hanging Oak. The large oak tree was a popular sight at the new courthouse, but as long-time sheriff Thomas A. Binford said, the executions of criminals took place in the rafters of the jail and not at the oak tree. Nevertheless, the more exhilarating story of a hanging oak has captured the imagination of some folks, and the plaque was placed by the tree."

So maybe instead of the Old Hanging Oak, it should be known as the "Old Hanging Around to Hear the Verdict Oak."

45

SLANTED CITY

Why don't downtown Houston roads run north-south and east-west ?

Most people who've never seen downtown Houston on a map have to look twice. Rather than a basic north–south–east–west orientation, the city looks crooked—like it's sliding downhill. Highways are listed as going north or south, but near downtown, Highway 69 goes from northeast to southwest and Interstate 45 runs from northwest to southeast. Even Interstate 10, which basically runs east-west from California to Florida, takes a crooked little dip in downtown Houston. C'mon, what gives?

The answer lies with one early member of the Borden family (of Borden milk fame). Expert historian Louis Aulbach explains: "The streets of the city lie at about 35 degrees off due north (to the east). The Allen brothers made no comment about why the alignment was that way. Historians generally have suggested that the alignment was designed to maximize the use of the waterfront for the city wharves. Yet, there is really no proof for such a claim. The late James Glass, a local historian and map designer, told me his idea on the reason the city was laid out the way it is.

"Glass knew the Allen brothers wanted to make money by selling town lots, as well as other tracts of land, as the town grew as a commercial center. When Gail Borden surveyed the proposed town site, he saw one major topographic feature on the site that was problematic: a gully cut across the area, right through the center of the town, making several blocks and lots less than ideal for sale. However, if the plat of the blocks were aligned so that the gully ran down the right-of-way of one of the streets, the number of 'poor' lots could be minimized. The gully was then aligned with the right-of-way of Carolina Street (later renamed

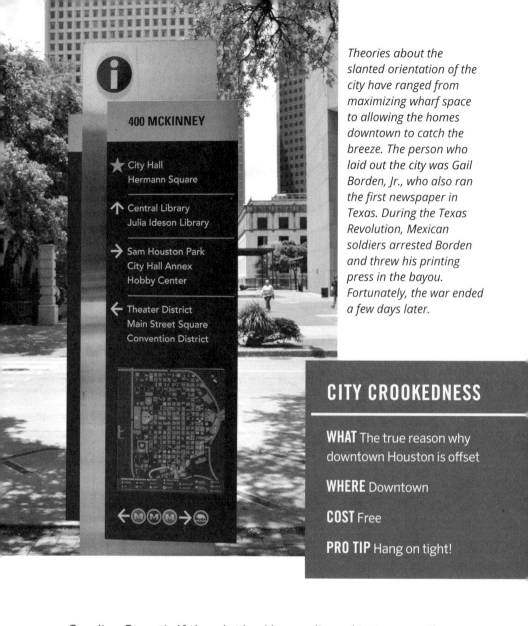

400 MCKINNEY

★ City Hall
Hermann Square

↑ Central Library
Julia Ideson Library

→ Sam Houston Park
City Hall Annex
Hobby Center

← Theater District
Main Street Square
Convention District

Theories about the slanted orientation of the city have ranged from maximizing wharf space to allowing the homes downtown to catch the breeze. The person who laid out the city was Gail Borden, Jr., who also ran the first newspaper in Texas. During the Texas Revolution, Mexican soldiers arrested Borden and threw his printing press in the bayou. Fortunately, the war ended a few days later.

CITY CROOKEDNESS

WHAT The true reason why downtown Houston is offset

WHERE Downtown

COST Free

PRO TIP Hang on tight!

Caroline Street). If the plat had been aligned to true north, the gully would have cut diagonally across several city blocks, ruining a large number of prime lots."

"The alignment of the original Houston city streets has puzzled people for decades," says expert historian Louis Aulbach.

46

WHISPERS, RIBBITS, AND MORE

What hidden secrets were built into Rice University's buildings?

So you know about Valhalla (page 74), because it's hard to keep a secret involving cheap beer. But the Rice campus has more surprises to offer than a few cold ones and a heated discussion about the true meaning of "postmodernism." Many of these hidden Easter eggs can be found in the school's architecture.

Probably the most famous of the school's secret building features is the Frog Wall, which is a bit of the façade at the Rice School of Architecture's M. D. Anderson Hall. Bordering the doorway from the main quad, you'll see a strip of indentations; run your finger down them and they sound like a frog's ribbit. Some say they're just a random aesthetic feature that makes the noise as a happy accident. Others say they're an homage to the frogs displaced when the campus was built during 1911 and 1912. But one thing's for sure: it's probably not an homage to the TCU Horned Frogs.

Another hidden bit of fun around Rice is the whispering alcoves found in the doorway leading into Herzstein Hall (the old physics building). Two people can whisper quietly into opposite sides of the wall and hear each other clearly. While you're there, check out the bizarre door handles carved to resemble some kind of evil dolphin or something.

Anderson Hall was built in 1947, designed by architects Staub & Rather, in consultation with Architecture School Chairman William Ward Watkin.

It's the little round holes that make the "ribbit" sound. Scary Sasquatch arm not included.

FROG WALL

WHAT Froggy-sounding architectural flourish

WHERE Rice University's M. D. Anderson Hall

COST Free

PRO TIP The university has a great jogging loop, too.

Not sure what the deal is with those, but they're creepy as all get out.

Also interesting are the many adornments that feature people who were still alive and working at the school when it was built. One example is an image carved into a column of the chemistry building depicting chemistry professor (and later Dean) Harry Boyer Weiser as a dragon mauling a student while his assistant looks on. There's even a carving of the school's original architect on the architecture building with a group of students bowing down to him. Illuminati confirmed.

47

HOUSE OF SCRIBES

How did a nondescript home in Montrose become a powerhouse for global literature?

The homes on the 1500 block of West Main in Montrose are established and stately, with broad tree canopies and well-manicured lawns. The area is home to successful professionals, art lovers, and the upwardly mobile. But the two-story brick house at 1520 W. Main has all kinds of dreamy-eyed characters coming and going. They're worse than a cult; they're writers. The house is scribe central for Inprint, Houston's premier nonprofit organization in the literary arts.

With a mission to inspire Houston's readers and writers, Inprint is a champion of how creating and appreciating quality fiction, poetry, and creative nonfiction can have an impact on all Houstonians. Inside the walls of the house, the group holds workshops wherein everyday people can hone their craft over an eight- to ten-week period with the guidance of their instructor and the feedback of their peers.

The instructors are selected from the prestigious University of Houston Creative Writing Program, which admits only six to eight students each year. The workshops are modeled on graduate-level courses, and they are a great way to find your pathway to publication. They also host a First Friday Poetry Series and open mic, a book club, and the Inprint Poetry Buskers, who write poetry on demand in public (if you haven't seen this, it's amazing).

They also bring big names to town for the Inprint Margarett Root Brown Reading Series. We're talking names like Salman Rushdie, John Irving, John Updike, and Sandra Cisneros, to name a few. In addition, they also provide fellowships and other financial support for up-and-coming writers. So if you live on West Main, please be patient with

Author Jason Reynolds signs at the Meyerland Performing and Visual Arts Middle School as part of the Inprint Cool Brains! Reading Series. The fan in the foreground is presumably Spider-Man, who does whatever a spider can. Photo courtesy of Inprint.

the starry-eyed dreamers stumbling in and out of the house with their worn-out copies of *Gulf Coast* and *The New Yorker*. They're on a journey. There's no telling where they'll end up and, for many, it started at that house.

Neighborhood disturbances involving structuralism, the value of rhyme scheme, and the Oxford comma have not been substantiated.

48

DOWNTOWN'S CAPITOL

Do you know the Republic-era history that lies at the heart of Main & Texas?

Main Street and Texas Avenue is the heart of downtown, home to the iconic Rice Apartments (formerly the Rice Hotel) and its lavish Crystal Ballroom. But before it was the Rice, did you know that land actually housed the capitol of the Republic of Texas?

On the exact spot where the Rice Apartments stand today, a wood-frame building served as Texas' capitol building from 1837 to 1839. It didn't much resemble the stately, high-tech granite castle of today's state capitol, but it's where Sam Houston, Mirabeau B. Lamar, and other Texas leaders conducted the business of the nation.

Texas earned its independence from Mexico in 1836 and was its own nation until being annexed into the United States in 1845. Houston was the capital of Texas before Austin. In fact, headquarters hopped around a lot in the years after the Texas Revolution. Houston might still be the Texas capital if it weren't for a forty-four-year-old woman named Angelina Eberly.

The capital was moved to Houston temporarily because of fears that the Mexican Army would reinvade. H-Town seemed more easily protected, but people in Austin were afraid that if they let the move go too long then it would stick. In a conflict known as the Archives War, a team of

RICE APARTMENTS

WHAT Site of Former Texas Capitol

WHERE Main Street and Texas Avenue

COST Free

PRO TIP Check out the placards on the old red streetlights in front of the Rice, which tell the story of the old capitol building.

The Texas flag still flies proudly on the land, although the Texas capitol building is long gone. John F. Kennedy spent his last night at the Rice before his assassination on November 22, 1963.

rangers transferring the state papers were intercepted by Austin vigilantes. Angelina Eberly actually fired a cannon at the rangers making the delivery. Figuring they had better things to do than scuffle over paperwork, the rangers turned over the archives and went home.

Houston's capitol building was razed in 1881, and the new building eventually became the first Rice Hotel. Jesse Jones bought the building, razed the old Rice, and built the current Rice Hotel in its spot where the Texas capitol once stood. Today the Texas State Capitol is in the Segway-laden streets of Hipster Central.

Houston was named "temporary capital of the Republic of Texas" upon winning the Texas Revolution, and a capitol building was erected at Main Street and Texas Avenue. But Houston was a rough city, full of brawling, dueling, drunkenness, and prostitution. Between that and the Yellow Fever, the politicians eventually ran for the hills.

49

PASSAGE TO INDIA

What's that exotic looking building off Avenue E in Stafford?

Just east of Sugar Land's River Bend Country Club you'll see something that looks like a temple from a foreign land. And with good reason—that's exactly what it is. A mandir is a place of worship for those who follow the Hindu faith, and Houston's BAPS Shri Swaminarayan Mandir was the first traditionally built mandir in North America.

Open to people of all faiths and completely free to visit, the mandir serves as a temple, a community center, and a gateway for visitors to learn about Hinduism and Indian culture.

The building is made from thirty-three thousand pieces of hand-carved Italian Carrara marble and Turkish limestone sculpted by mandir craftsmen who specialize in creating these unique buildings. Artists made each piece of the temple in India according to the Shilpa Shastra, the ancient Sanskrit guidelines of creation for arts, crafts, and architecture. Next, the pieces of the building were sent to Texas, where specialists from India put it all together. It took four years to build the foundation and eighteen months to assemble all the intricate pieces and build the structure itself.

Fun fact: 15.1% of the world's population is Hindu. The oldest Hindu temples are ancient, and many are found outside India. The Mundeshwari Devi Temple, for example, in India's state of Bihar, dates back to AD 625. Cambodia's Angkor Wat was originally a Hindu temple.

BAPS SHRI SWAMINARAYAN MANDIR

WHAT First traditional Hindu Mandir in North America

WHERE 1150 Brand Ln.

COST Free

PRO TIP Hit the Shayona Café (vegetarian), as well as the sweets and snack shop, for a traditional nosh.

Traditional mandirs are designed and constructed based on ancient rules and precepts. More than thirty-three thousand individual pieces were shipped to Houston from India and carefully assembled on site.

Although a thin wall of trees masks it somewhat from the road, Shri Swaminarayan Mandir sits on twenty-two acres of well-tended gardens and fountains. A large reflection pool stands in front of the mandir, swaying palm trees line the grounds, and manicured lawns stretch across the campus. It's a peaceful place, meant to inspire, bring people together, and promote contemplation.

Visitors to the mandir can explore the amazing temple, leave an offering to the gods, attend a lecture, take classes, and stop by the gift shop for a souvenir. You can learn more about the Hindu faith and Indian culture, and check out the mandir's amazing architecture and construction. There is no substitute for seeing the ornate carvings in the building itself to truly appreciate their craftsmanship—evocative depictions of the gods, elaborate shapes and patterns, delicate borders, and grand archways. And, of course, there's no better place to experience Diwali.

117

What, uh, remains of the old 1840 City Cemetery?

Glenwood. Congregation Beth Israel. The old Founders Cemetery. Although there are a number of celebrated cemeteries in town, many people don't know about the old city cemetery built in 1840.

The old 1840 Houston City Cemetery was at Elder and Girard, just north of the Theater District. It was sectioned out depending on who you were: everyday people, Freemasons, Confederate Veterans, and even a "Potter's Field" for "criminals, suicides and persons killed in a duel," as its historical placard proclaims. It's believed that up to ten thousand people were buried in the cemetery, which was only about five acres in size.

As Houston grew, and despite citizen pushback, the City of Houston built Jefferson Davis Hospital right on top of some of the cemetery. Next, it built a fire department maintenance facility on another part. The area kept being developed, and today there's not much aboveground evidence left.

In recent years, anthropologists have engaged with the site to help unlock some of its past. They've found what appears to be some pretty astonishing archaeological evidence: pirates!

Jefferson Davis hospital was built on top of Houston's first city-owned cemetery. A section of the Houston Fire Department facility next door still preserves some of the original graves and reburied remains. The site once held an obelisk and bronze marker honoring Confederate veterans, but those have been removed over the years.

The old 1840 Municipal Cemetery was Houston's first city-owned cemetery. Now all that remains of the old cemetery (above ground, anyway) is some concrete curbing.

OLD 1840 HOUSTON CITY CEMETERY

WHAT Site of a long-forgotten cemetery filled with Confederate soldiers

WHERE Girard and Elder Sts.

COST Free

PRO TIP The Elder Street Artist Lofts is private property and a working art space, so if you visit the area please do not disturb the artists.

Yep, evidence was found in and around an estimated forty "black earth" graves, complete with pottery samples similar to the types used by English settlers in the 1600s. The theory is that a group of privateer settlers was granted land rights along the Gulf by King Charles I of England and created a failed colony—the remains of which lay beneath the old 1840 Houston City Cemetery.

Does this land really hold previously unknown keys to Houston's past? Who knows? During the archaeologists' study of the site, a parking lot was paved right over the area of study. Today, Jeff Davis Hospital is the Elder Street Artist Lofts.

We're not saying this land is haunted. We're just saying that if any place were haunted, an abandoned graveyard containing possibly hundreds of dead Confederate soldiers, former slaves, and pirates—which was built upon by property developers and currently hosts a defunct hospital—seems like a pretty good candidate.

51

DISMOUNTED DOWNTIME

Where do HPD patrol horses go when not on duty?

You've seen them downtown. You've seen them working crowd control. You've seen them in Hermann Park. They're the Houston Police Department Mounted Patrol, thirty-eight horses (as of this writing) and their mounted patrol officers who help keep Houston's streets safe. The horses include a mix of Percherons, Belgiums, Tennessee Walkers, Hanoverians, and Dutch Warmbloods.

Where do all those horses go when they're not on patrol? Not Buffalo Wild Wings or a Brazilian Jiu Jitsu class. As it turns out, they go to a big barn, stable, and training complex just off Little York Road on the north side. This pristine 15-acre campus treats these horse heroes in style with forty-six generously sized stalls in which they can lounge, a 5.5-acre turnout pasture, an outside run, a veterinary area, an air-conditioned tack room, and heaters for the winter.

Most people don't know about the complex—and even fewer know that Houstonians can visit the stable and feed the horses.

Yep, you can stop by the barn and feed these four-legged flatfoots a carrot or apple or some peppermint candy. The officers prefer that you buy the treats from them (it's super-cheap, around $3) so that they can control what the horses eat. After all, these animals need to stay in shape to help serve and protect.

HPD horses are always in demand. Officers can hardly make it from Point A to Point B without citizens stopping

---

When the Houston Police Department's thirty-eight horses aren't out keeping the streets safe, they're at a barn just off Little York—and you can go visit them.

You can't miss the horse barn, with its giant horse out front. Remember, as the website states, horses can't distinguish carrots from fingers, so please feed them the former and not the latter.

HOUSTON POLICE DEPARTMENT MOUNTED PATROL

WHAT Home to Houston's hero horses

WHERE 5005 Little York Rd.

COST $3

PRO TIP If you want to visit on weekends, you have to call ahead: (832) 394-0394.

them for a horse selfie. And when not on duty, they're galloping around doing demonstrations for various groups. Citizens even adopt them, earning sponsors the right to name the horse and have their name or company logo displayed on the horse's stall.

When a horse is retired from service, whoever sponsored it is given the first opportunity to take it in. If that's not possible, there is a long list of people waiting to adopt former HPD horses. Hey, everyone loves a hero.

<u>52</u> THE WRIGHT STUFF

What's so special about the house at 12020 Tall Oaks Street in Bunker Hill?

There are a lot of beautiful homes in Bunker Hill Village— a quiet, verdant section of West Houston. But one in particular stands out to fans of contemporary architecture. That's because it has a very cool secret: it's the only home in Houston designed by iconic American architect Frank Lloyd Wright.

The Thaxton House is one of just three homes that Wright designed in Texas; the others are in Dallas and Amarillo. The home was built in 1955 for William L. Thaxton, Jr., an insurance executive. The neighborhood was much less developed at the time, with Bunker Hill Village having only been incorporated a year earlier. Before that, the area was mostly just sawmills and the odd home or two. It was originally built on 1.2 acres.

Many consider the 1,800-square-foot Thaxton House as a prime example of Wright's Usonian style. With big windows, natural wood, concrete block walls, red stained concrete floors, and a fireplace big enough to step inside, the home carries a number of Wright's signature residential touches. It even had original furniture that was secured to the floor.

Frank Lloyd Wright was born in Wisconsin just after the War between the States. Following his passion, he would go on to design 1,114 architectural works—effectively changing the way Americans design, build, and live. Nature was a big influence on his work. "Study nature," he said, "love nature, stay close to nature. It will never fail you."

Over the years, various owners had modified the original design with columns and all kinds of off-brand changes— including ripping out all the original built-in furniture. But in 1991 architectural aficionados Drs. Betty Lee and Allen

Frank Lloyd Wright coined the term "Usonian" to describe his concept of streamlined and inspired middle-class living. Built with economic construction and natural materials, he worked closely with residents when designing them, and named each Usonian house after its owner. Photo courtesy of the Library of Congress.

WILLIAM L. THAXTON, JR. HOUSE

WHAT Houston's only home designed by Frank Lloyd Wright

WHERE 12020 Tall Oaks St.

COST $2.9 million when last listed (as of this writing)

PRO TIP This is someone's house so, you know, don't go creeping around and making it weird.

F. Gaw bought the house, working with the prestigious firm Kirksey to both build on and painstakingly restore it to the original spirit. As of this writing, Thaxton House's most recent list price was $2.9 million.

This Bunker Hill Village home is the only example of Frank Lloyd Wright's residential work in Houston, and one of only three Wright-designed homes in the entire state of Texas.

53

BATTLE FOR THE BUCKLE

Did you know that rodeo food vendors are competing behind the scenes?

The Houston Livestock Show and Rodeo (HLSR) is one of the biggest events in town. In 2019, attendance topped 75,000 on multiple days—the George Strait concert netted a record 80,020 people (I was there, and it was awesome). Everybody's got their own favorite thing to do at the rodeo, and for a lot of people that thing is to try out all the interesting foods: from fried Oreos to turkey legs to Something Unexpected On a Stick. I just made that last one up, but something at every fair-type event is always on a stick. No secrets there.

But did you know that while you're going about your business eating your way around NRG Stadium, those same food vendors are battling for a prestigious behind-the-scenes honor?

The Golden Buckle Foodie Awards confer a number of prizes on rodeo food vendors from all around the event who enter their favorite signature dishes. And it's quite an honor. First, the vendor picks their most delicious dish to present to a panel of celebrity judges, who nosh through it all in a few hours. Winners are then picked in categories such as Best Food on a Stick, Best New Flavor, Best Fried Food, and Most Creative Food.

While you're lazily walking around the rodeo looking at the animals and waiting for the concert to start, food vendors from around the country are battling for the prestigious Golden Buckle Foodie Awards.

At the time of this writing, the Best Fried Food—tough competition at the Rodeo—went to The Original Minneapple Pie's "Minnechocolate Pie." The Secret Houston team will be on the lookout for this one next year. Photo courtesy of the Houston Livestock Show and Rodeo.

BEHIND THE SCENES BUCKLE

WHAT Golden Buckle Foodie Awards

WHERE Houston Livestock Show and Rodeo

COST Varies per item

PRO TIP Try them all! And get your step count in to offset the calories.

Big bragging rights are at, uhm, steak here. But for the general rodeo-going public, everybody wins. Visitors can stop by a special booth and register to take on eating the goods of all eight category winners. Slurp 'em all down and you'll get cool prizes like T-shirts, koozies, and other stuff—like maybe a gym membership.

The winners in 2019 included Holmes Smokehouse and its "Bacon Wrapped Pecan Smoked Sausage" for Best Food on a Stick, the Totally Baked Cookie Joint with its "Smoorcookie" for Best New Flavor, and The Candy Factory for both its "Hot Crunchy Cheetos Cotton Candy" as best Classic Fair Food and its "Unicorn Float" as Most Creative Food.

54

HOUSTON'S JUICIEST SECRET

Did anyone ever love oranges as much as Jeff McKissack?

Houston postal worker Jeff McKissack loved oranges. Like, really, really, loved them. So much so, in fact, that he bought two adjacent lots next to his home on Munger Street and built a monument to the fruit.

Born in 1902, Jefferson Davis McKissack drove a truck during the Great Depression. Those were hard times for most, and many were unsure of their next meal. McKissack spent those years trucking Florida oranges around the Southeast. His passion for the orange blossomed—especially regarding its health benefits. He felt strongly about the energy, health, and vitality that came from the nutritious fruit. And he lived the brand, working hard well into old age to transform his passion for the peel into what is today an off-the-beaten-path landmark.

Resembling an old-school State Fair exhibit, the Orange Show is a folk art environment that incorporates found materials to create a number of exhibits praising what McKissack believed was the perfect food.

A multi-level affair with Texas and U.S. flags flying overhead, there's no missing it. The space features metalwork, statues, tractor seats and wheels, brickwork, woodland creatures, birds, and a number of themed installations featuring everything from dinosaurs to Santa Claus—all in praise of the orange. Forget budgets and grant money. McKissack found or collected all building materials on the cheap, and he did it all solo.

A bit of poetry on display at the Orange Show: "Woodman, Spare That Tree!" by George Pope Morris. The first stanza, anyway.

McKissack worked on the project from 1956 until 1980. Sadly, he died of a stroke shortly after it opened, but a caring arts patron stepped in and formed a nonprofit organization to preserve this bit of folk art amazingness—and big time H-Town bucks followed. Today, it's not just the Orange Show but the Orange Show Center for Visionary Art, enabling all sorts of creative self-expression, from this fruity showcase to the popular Houston Art Car Parade.

McKissack was right after all: oranges really can fuel great things.

On Munger Street just east of the University of Houston, Jefferson Davis McKissack built this shrine to the humble orange and to the power of positive thinking and healthy living.

Did you know there used to be a Confederate prison camp where UHD is today?

The University of Houston–Downtown has helped Houstonians improve their prospects for more than forty years. Many people know that the school is housed in the art deco 1930 Merchants and Manufacturers Building. This rare architectural survivor in a downtown notoriously unkind to historical buildings was once praised as "a modern miracle of architectural genius" and brings character to the area.

Fewer people know of that land's gray past. Before serving as an ambitious, multimodal hub of commerce, the land on which the M&M Building stands once housed a prisoner of war camp for the Confederate States of America.

Although its role in the war was mainly logistical, Texas did play a part in the War between the States. Almost ninety thousand Texans actively fought for the Confederacy, although the idea of secession was contentious here at home. Sam Houston was ardently anti-secession, but his was not a popular sentiment at the time and much of the South's Trans-Mississippi Department was run from Houston. Union ships pounded the coastline, putting everyone on edge. It was a turbulent, violent time filled with hardship, hate, and loss.

The northside confluence of White Oak Bayou and Buffalo Bayou at Main Street housed a warehouse complex that was transformed into a prison camp upon the war's outbreak. The majority of those held at the facility were 42nd Massachusetts volunteers captured during the Battle of Galveston. About 350 men from the battle were housed at the camp. Enlisted men were kept under tight watch, although Northern officers were free to roam the city on their word of honor that they would not escape. True to the

Today's University of Houston–Downtown campus. The 1930 M&M Building in which it is housed is a fantastic bit of art deco architecture designed by the firm of Giesecke & Harris.

PRISONERS OF THE PAST

WHAT Former Confederate Prison Camp

WHERE 1 Main St.

COST Free

PRO TIP Swing by Allen's Landing while you're down there (but do it in the daytime).

abhorrent practices of the day, Northern soldiers of color were either sold as slaves or sent to Huntsville.

In 1965, a Texas Historical Commission marker commemorating the camp was placed at 150 Girard Street, where the UHD campus now stands.

The Merchants and Manufacturers Building, today the University of Houston–Downtown, was built on land that once housed a Confederate prison camp.

You want to cast a spell on someone but need the supplies. Where's the secret spot to get what you need?

The Magick Cauldron bills itself as Houston's premier Pagan religious supplier—carrying everything from altar pentacles and witch's cauldrons to special lunar candles, tarot cards, and rune sets. It's a fun place to visit, since the average person doesn't often encounter things like skull candles or books about crystals and auras. They've got a lot of stuff: about twenty thousand things in the shop, including three thousand book titles.

Now, just to be clear, this isn't some cheesy party supply store where you go to get that black, pointy witch's hat for the office Halloween party. This is the place actual witches go to buy all the robes and oils and other things they need to practice witchcraft. More than thirty years old, the business has become a fixture for Houston occultists.

Don't believe in witches? Well, they believe in themselves, apparently. *Newsweek* reports that there may be as many as 1.5 million practicing Wiccans in the United States. The Magick Cauldron even sells little beginner's Port-a-Witch kits that include candles, incense, a ceremonial dagger and more—all in a little wooden box that serves as an altar. For tarot cards, you can get them new (recommended) or used

The Magick Cauldron is ground zero for Pagan supplies here in town. The word *pagan* is said to have come from the Latin *paganus*, meaning "a rustic or country person." In a religious context, it once referred to a rural villager who stuck to worshipping the old gods.

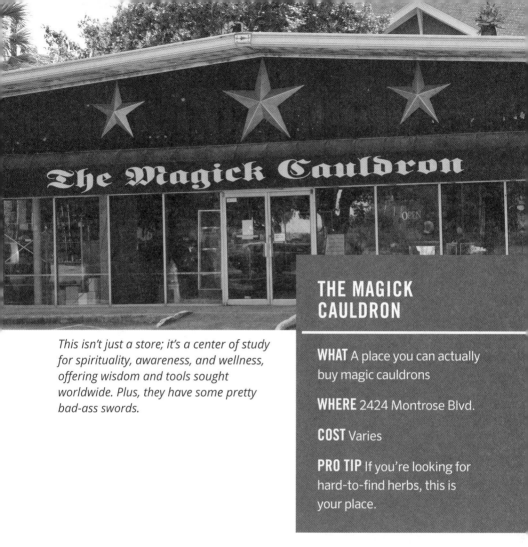

This isn't just a store; it's a center of study for spirituality, awareness, and wellness, offering wisdom and tools sought worldwide. Plus, they have some pretty bad-ass swords.

THE MAGICK CAULDRON

WHAT A place you can actually buy magic cauldrons

WHERE 2424 Montrose Blvd.

COST Varies

PRO TIP If you're looking for hard-to-find herbs, this is your place.

and cleaned with a spiritual cleansing, which also sounds like what I need to do to my truck at this point.

Even if you positively don't want anything to do with alternative spirituality, the Magick Cauldron has all kinds of other cool stuff. Books run the gamut of non-witchy topics that include Kundalini, the Kabbalah, self-help, herbalism, and general health. There are some sweet Medieval weapons and armor, cool Steampunk gear, handcrafted jewelry, and really anything you need for authentic Renfest paraphernalia.

Come for the sorcery, stay for the swords.

⁵⁷ DARK WATERS

Every wonder how many people have parked in the bayou permanently?

You see all kinds of interesting things in the bayou, ranging from catfish and turtles to alligator gar and waterfowl. But one secret nobody talks about is the number of cars and trucks that wind up in the bayou. It's an unsettling thought, but it makes sense. After all, in a city of millions without much public transportation, there are going to be some throwaways. And that's not even considering the auto-apocalypse that inevitably ensues when a major hurricane blows through.

Widespread knowledge and concern about the vehicles began in 2011 when an elderly woman went missing. The Houston Police Department asked the Texas EquuSearch Mounted Search and Recovery Team, the volunteer group that helps find missing people on horseback, to search the water for the woman using their sonar-equipped boats in 2012. Along the way, the group found a car underwater. Then another, and another. Eventually, it mapped 127 vehicles submerged in various bayous around town.

Authorities say that most of the cars submerged in Houston bayous are stolen and abandoned. It was feared that some might have become the de facto graves of unlucky Houstonians who drove into the water accidentally—or wound up there under even darker circumstances.

To address the problem, a pilot project was assembled in 2016 between the Harris County Flood Control District and the Houston Police Department, removing a number of the vehicles. Harris County Precinct 2 Commissioner Jack Morman joined the others in a second round of removals in 2017. Contracting a marine salvage company and towing

A "No Motor Vehicles" sign posted along Buffalo Bayou at Wilcrest Drive. Turn around, don't drown.

CARS IN THE BAYOU

WHAT 100+ submerged vehicles

WHERE Underwater

COST Insurance deductible

PRO TIP Keep it on the road!

service, the cars were lifted out using inflatable bags to float them to the top, where a heavy towing truck would cable them out and haul them away.

No bodies have been found in the recovery efforts.

The oldest car removed in the recent recovery initiative was a 1978 Datsun 280Z reported stolen in 1982. Whether there was a Hall & Oates cassette tape in its stereo was neither confirmed nor denied by authorities.

58

DOME SWEET HOME

Did you know that "Judge" Roy Hofheinz had his own private apartment in the Astrodome?

Until Roy Hofheinz built the Astrodome from 1962 to 1965, there was no such thing as an indoor sports stadium. Home of the team originally called the Colt .45s (today the Astros), the dome was the world's first all air-conditioned stadium. It was also dubbed "the Eighth Wonder of the World." Mickey Mantle hit Major League Baseball's first indoor home run in the Astrodome.

The stadium was national news when it opened. People talked about the exciting new baseball franchise. They talked about the big shot judge and real estate developer who made it all happen and the amusement park he built across the street. They talked about the "spacemen" dressed as astronauts who picked up the litter on the field, and how President Lyndon B. Johnson and his wife attended the first game. But not many talked about the "secret" apartment and offices Hofheinz built upstairs.

Hofheinz was a colorful character. Born in Beaumont, he was just nineteen when he graduated from law school. House of Representatives. Harris County Judge. Two terms as Houston Mayor. He knew who to push and who to pitch to get things done, and his bringing Major League Baseball, and the Astrodome, to Houston proved his prowess.

Hofheinz's Astrodome hideaway included an elaborate office, a bar covered in red velvet, a men's barber shop, a women's beauty salon, a private playroom for his children, a bowling alley and putting green, a carnival-style shooting gallery, a small church-like space, and a number of "sky rooms" from which you could look out onto the field—and maybe shoot a game of pool.

The stairway up to Hofheinz's private suite at the Astrodome. This picture was taken in the late 1980s when his private spaces were opened up to clear them out and make room for extra seating. Media was invited to document the space (hence the guy's camera). Photo from the *Houston Post* collection at the Houston Metropolitan Research Center.

SECRET SUITES

WHAT The Judge's behind-the-scenes Astrodome apartment

WHERE Sold out to make more seating

COST Not open to the public as of this writing

PRO TIP Keep up with the latest Astrodome revitalization plans.

The parties, deals, and who-knows-what-else that went on in the Judge's private palace are pure speculation for most of us. But even the best parties end. Hofheinz died in 1982 of a heart attack, and his private apartment was demolished to make way for extra seating. As of this writing, the Astrodome is still standing but abandoned.

Did you know that the creator of the Astrodome, Roy "The Judge" Hofheinz, kept a number of elaborate personal rooms, offices, and entertainment spaces in the 'dome?

59

BODIES OF KNOWLEDGE

Where can Houstonians go to learn all about the secrets inside us?

Though we all have a body, many of us don't know that much about how it actually works. There's no owner's manual; we just have to figure it out, like someone trying to find the windshield wipers on a new car. Fortunately, there's one place in Houston that can get you inside the human body—and do it in a fun and interesting way: The Health Museum.

One of the best kept secrets in Houston's Museum District, the Health Museum's mission is to foster wonder and curiosity about health, medical science, and the human body. Technically called the John P. McGovern Museum of Health & Medical Science, the museum has its roots in the 1962 campaign "Victory Over Polio" and a resulting effort from the Harris County Medical Society to create a series of public health exhibits.

Today, it's one of the most interesting and interactive human body experiences in the nation—giving visitors a larger-than-life journey through the body. The museum's Amazing Body Gallery lets you learn how your body works through an outsized walk-through tour, which is really cool. The exhibit has a walk-through brain, a huge eyeball, an interactive heart wall, and much more. The museum has

---

Sleep. The immune system. The brain-body connection. The human body is one of the world's most fascinating mysteries, and this place helps you explore these wonders. Granted, some bodies are more fascinating than others.

The mission of the John P. McGovern Museum of Health & Medical Science is to foster wonder and curiosity about health, medical science, and the human body.

THE HEALTH MUSEUM

WHAT Your body's inner-most secrets

WHERE 1515 Hermann Dr.

COST $10 Adults, $8 for kids over 3

PRO TIP Check out the calorie crank to see exactly how hard it is to work off that milkshake.

also featured traveling exhibits from the American Museum of Natural History's "The Secret World Inside You."

Located right next to the Children's Museum, this is an especially great place for kids to learn about health and the body. After all, children are the future—and they haven't yet gotten into the habit of coming home from a long day at the office only to polish off a sack of goodies from Brothers Taco House and three cans of Sam's Daily (as a random example). Kids visiting the museum can see a giant brain, assemble a skeleton digitally, measure how loud they can scream—and even run through a disturbingly lifelike representation of the human colon (ew).

60 THE MAN BEHIND THE SCAN

Just who the heck was M. D. Anderson anyway?

People come to Houston from all around the world to fight cancer at the University of Texas M. D. Anderson Cancer Center. But just who is the man behind this prestigious institution of healing and learning? Some Nobel Prize-winning physician? Perhaps an inventor of medical technology? A groundbreaking pathologist, perhaps? Nope.

He was actually a banker and cotton merchant from Jackson, Tennessee.

Monroe Dunaway Anderson was born in 1873. The son of a local bank president, he also went into banking. But in his early thirties, Anderson decided to go into the cotton business with a few other family members. The firm they created—Anderson, Clayton & Company—would eventually be named by *Fortune* magazine as the "largest buyer, seller, storer, and shipper of raw cotton in the world."

In 1916, Anderson, Clayton & Company moved its

Everyone knows the hospital, but nobody knows the name. As it turns out, M. D. Anderson was a wealthy cotton broker.

The University of Texas M. D. Anderson Cancer Center at 1515 Holcombe. There are no guarantees in the medical world, but they did save my life a few years back.

headquarters to Houston because of the city's prominence in the industry and proximity to Galveston's port infrastructure. The company grew to have subsidiaries that included a Mexican bank, a barge line, a foods division, and a number of insurance companies.

Anderson had become a titan of industry, but he never married or had a family. In his later years, he wanted to give back and protect his hard-won business interests from looting by the federal government upon his death. So in 1936 he created the M. D. Anderson Foundation—a charitable foundation run by a few friends who'd been long-trusted legal advisors.

Anderson passed away in 1939, but his name lives on in the hearts of cancer survivors everywhere. In 1941, when the state legislature appropriated a half-million dollars for the establishment of a cancer research hospital, the M. D. Anderson Foundation trustees jumped on it—matching funds and locking in the site for Houston. This foundation would lay the groundwork for the Texas Medical Center, today the largest medical center in the world.

⁶¹ FREE PARKING

Do you know the secret to free parking at Astros home games?

What? Free parking for the 'stros? These days, parking to see these World Series champs can run you up to $75 downtown, right? And that's not including the cost of paying a homeless man $10 not to urinate on your SUV. But here's the secret workaround: Jackson Street Barbecue.

Jackson Street is the brainchild of Reef creator Bryan Caswell and Greg Gatlin of Gatlin's BBQ. On any given weekday, it's crawling with cops, suits, 'stros fans, and other denizens of downtown looking for a little downhome cookin' in the heart of the big city. Jackson Street serves up all of your favorites like brisket, sausage, pulled pork, burgers, and more—not to mention a Friday beef rib special so enormous that it looks like something they'd serve the Flintstones.

None of that is much of a secret, though. The secret is that when a baseball game rolls around, you can park in the lot at Jackson Street and Franklin Street right in front of the stadium for $50. This is about market price for nearby game parking, depending on who the Astros are playing. But the thing about this particular lot? Jackson Street Barbecue owns it. So if you park there, and only there, Jackson Street will give you a $50 food voucher.

So, basically, you can go downtown and eat $50 worth of sliced brisket, "yard bird," fried macaroni, and whatever

---

Not many people know about the secret deal from Jackson Street BBQ, in which you basically get free parking for Astros games. Or free food, however you want to think about it.

JACKSON STREET BBQ

WHAT Sweet Astros parking deal

WHERE 209 Jackson St.

COST $50

PRO TIP If it's a Friday game, try the beef ribs.

Jackson Street is just northeast of Minute Maid Park. Lock down your place early before the lot they own fills up.

else strikes your fancy. And then you get to slide next door and go see your Houston Astros win. All without really spending anything for parking. I mean, there's no such thing as a free lunch—but you have to park somewhere and eat somewhere anyway. So when you look at it that way, it really is like getting one or the other for free.

Plus, if the Astros lose, no other parking lot will help you drown your sorrows in jalapeño cheddar biscuits.

Who made those giant Presidential heads off Interstate 10 going into downtown?

Known colloquially as "Mount Rush Hour," these 18-foot depictions of Stephen F. Austin, Sam Houston, Abraham Lincoln, and George Washington are the work of Huntsville-born artist and sculptor David Adickes. Each bust sits upon a six-foot black block, upon which is collectively written "A Tribute to American Statesmanship." Technically, the plot of land they sit on is American Statesmanship Park, but the park is really just the statue sitting on a piece of land Adickes used to own.

Now in his 90s, Adickes is most famously known as the sculptor of the 67-foot statue of Sam Houston that stands off Interstate 45 in Huntsville, the artist's home town. Adickes studied art in Paris and then moved to Houston in the 1960s. Since then he's made a big impression on the H-Town art scene. Some love his work, and some hate it, but there's certainly no missing it.

American Statesmanship Park isn't far from Adickes's longtime studio on Summer Street—at the southwest corner of Interstates 45 and 69. A 35-foot statue of Charlie Chaplin and the heads of numerous American Presidents rise up from the property. There's no telling what type of outsized artwork you'll see at the Adickes studio, although rumor is that it's destined for demolition pending freeway development. It might be gone by the time this book comes

Often referred to as "Mount Rush Hour," the presidential busts on the side of Interstate 45 near downtown are the work of Huntsville-born artist David Adickes.

Washington and Lincoln in profile along the highway. The Oxford English Dictionary defines a statesman as a "skilled, experienced, and respected political leader or figure," so clearly Willie Nelson should be on the next iteration.

AMERICAN STATESMANSHIP PARK

WHAT Larger-than-life roadside art

WHERE 1400 Elder St.

COST Free

PRO TIP You'll have to get creative with parking if too many people visit at once.

out. Other visible works around town include the iconic "We Love Houston" sign or 36-foot statues of The Beatles.

Known in H-Town for his sculpture, Adickes is also an accomplished painter. His paintings often fetch thousands at auction. Citing Picasso, Chagall, and Braque as inspirations, he's cranked out a *ton* of distinctive and engaging work over the years. Next time you drive by the stately faces of Mount Rush Hour, think not only of the statesmen but also of the many hardworking artists in Houston looking to make their own mark.

63 OFFICERS AND GENTLEMEN

Just what was the Houston Light Guard?

If you've ever visited the Buffalo Soldiers National Museum at 3816 Caroline Street, you'll notice its distinctive old building. It's a good fit for the museum, which serves as a research center for American history and the legacy of the African American soldier. But this was not the building's original function. Before its service as a museum, it was an armory for a citizen fighting force called the Houston Light Guard.

The Houston Light Guard was a local militia assembled in 1873 by prominent Houstonians. Today the word *militia* conjures images of weekend warriors or political extremists listening to Alex Jones and living on the fringe. But back in the day, everyday people were called upon much more often to do tough jobs for the community—including occasional combat. Young men signed up out of a sense of community service. Around town, the Light Guard helped settle feuds, performed crowd control, kept the general peace, and even fought fires.

When not fighting, they drilled and marched. They marched and drilled. And then they drilled some more. Part fraternity and part corps, the group also served as a social club for well-off young men. Drill competitions were enthusiastically attended like today's football games, and the men won numerous military drill competitions.

Federal requirements eventually insisted that local units do two years in the regular army. That was a deal-breaker for these families, whose kids were expected to perform other duties. So the original Houston Light Guard disbanded, but was reactivated in 1898 to help occupy Cuba.

If you look above the entryway of the building, you can see reliefs featuring militiamen on duty. In more contemporary service, the Houston Light Guard fought Hitler's forces in seven campaigns across Africa and Europe.

YESTERDAY'S CITIZEN SOLDIERS

WHAT Former Light Guard Armory

WHERE 3816 Caroline St.

COST Free to see the building; $10 adult museum admission (free museum admission on Thursdays)

PRO TIP It's unrelated to the Houston Light Guard, but hit the museum inside for an engaging glimpse into the legacy of America's African-American soldiers.

In fact, Houston's volunteer fighting force, eventually designated Company G, 143rd Infantry, 72nd Brigade, 36th Division, was activated a number of times over the years. It deployed to the Rio Grande Valley when tensions with Mexico ran high, served in both world wars, and remained active until the Vietnam years.

Present arms!

Before it housed the Buffalo Soldiers National Museum, the building at Caroline and Truxillo Streets was once the armory for a local militia unit called the Houston Light Guard.

64

SURVIVAL OF THE SMARTEST

Whatever happened to the people and places of Enron?

Everybody who lived in Houston during the largest bankruptcy in U.S. history has their own story to tell about the 2001 Enron downfall. For many, the Enron scandal was a wrap when CEO Ken Lay and CFO Jeff Skilling were convicted of conspiracy and fraud in 2006. Ken Lay, the company's CEO at the time, died on July 5, 2006, from a heart attack. Conspiracy theories, rather cruel ones, still abound about his living the high life abroad.

In 2008, a class-action lawsuit filed by investors and shareholders was settled for $7.2 billion and paid out by a number of high-powered global banks implicated in the scandal.

Approximately sixteen people were sent to prison as a result of various financial malfeasances in connection with the scandal. Most are out of prison now. Jeff Skilling, Enron's CFO, was released from prison in February 2019. He's 65 today, and he served 12 years for fraud, conspiracy, and insider trading. In 2013, he reduced his sentence by 10 years as a result of giving up $42 million of his own money to fraud victims.

How about Enron's pipelines? Rich Kinder, who was at Enron when it was formed, bought a number of them. He

When it happened in 2001, the Enron bankruptcy was the largest in American history. Estimated losses totaled $74 billion, but many of its people and places are still around today.

The former Enron building at 1400 Smith is currently a Chevron office. Enron Field is now Minute Maid Park.

THE FORMER ENRON BUILDING

WHAT Where the smartest people in the room did business

WHERE 1400 Smith St.

COST Free

PRO TIP Buy low, sell high.

and a colleague snapped up $40 million worth of assets when the Enron ship went down. Today, Kinder Morgan has a market capitalization of somewhere around $44 billion. The president of the company's oil and gas subsidiary, Mark Papa, bought the company's oil and gas business for the bargain price of around $600 million. Today it's known as EOG Resources (as in Enron Oil and Gas) and is worth around $52.73 billion.

And the Enron building? Today it's occupied by Chevron. The big crooked "E" sign that once stood in front of the building was sold at auction in 2002 for $44,000. The newly sponsored sports stadium that Ken Lay helped spearhead, Enron Field, was rebranded as Minute Maid Park.

65

TUNNEL VISION

What is a mythical Mound, and how can you see one in the wild?

From the dog park to the Japanese garden, there's plenty to do at Hermann Park—not to mention the zoo and golf course and all the things around it. But for kids, a consistent favorite is the train. Since the late 1950s, this one-third-size replica of an 1863 C. P. Huntington steam train has been running kids in a two-mile loop around the park.

One of the most interesting sights for train riders is Destination Mound Town, which is an art installation painted within a train tunnel. The piece is a part of Trenton Doyle Hancock's fantastical *Moundverse* world.

Hancock, a prolific artist with a fantastic imagination and impressive oeuvre, features plant-like creatures called *Mounds*. The Mounds are the good guys in Hancock's world, constantly harassed by their enemies, the Vegans. In Hancock's world, the creatures date back fifty thousand years, and he's created numerous works within the Moundverse—each a surprisingly complex portrayal of bigger issues, such as morality and race.

Although he offers art beyond the Moundverse, Hancock's work has been building his Mound narrative for decades now—blending his own personal story with those of his mythical world. Born in Oklahoma City and raised in Paris, Texas, Hancock earned an MFA from the Tyler School of Art at Temple University. His work lives in the permanent collections of prestigious museums around the world,

MOUNDVERSE BY RAIL

WHAT Destination Mound Town

WHERE Hermann Park

COST $3.75 per train ride

PRO TIP Hit the pedal boats while you're there.

You'll see a variety of Hancock's creatures as you go through the "tunnel." You'll have to look quickly, though, as the train doesn't stop on the way through (at least, it didn't when the Secret Houston *team made the trip, and we did it twice).*

including the Museum of Modern Art in New York City. Today he calls Houston home.

Although technically you can see the mural without riding the train, it makes the park people nervous. They're afraid someone might be distracted by the wonder of the Moundverse and not notice a replica train barreling at them. So it's best to buy a train ticket—which you can pick up at the Hermann Park Lake Plaza. A round trip ride, which includes a run through Destination Mound Town, takes fifteen to twenty minutes.

In a long green metal shed at Hermann Park, artist Trenton Doyle Hancock invites passengers to explore the whimsical world of the Moundverse.

66

GHOST GUNS

What ever happened to the Twin Sisters of the Texas Revolution?

As Mexico's General Santa Anna marched north to crush the Texas Revolution in 1836, he had a proper army: uniforms, weapons, and even a 150-person marching band. The Texan forces were merely settlers fighting, for the most part, with whatever weapons were a part of their everyday lives.

But Texas had people working full-time to lobby for U.S. support. One of those lobbyists, Francis Smith, convinced the town of Cincinnati to finance, manufacture, and donate two six-pound iron cannons to the Texan cause. After much logistical jiggery-pokery, the cannons eventually caught up with Texan forces at the Battle of San Jacinto.

Filled with a hardscrabble ammunition of horseshoes, broken glass, and other on-hand items, the guns led the troops into a surprise assault that caught the Mexican forces off guard at the Battle of San Jacinto. A monument to the Twin Sisters stands on the battleground today. After the revolution, the guns were sent to Austin during the brief attempted Mexican invasion of the Republic of Texas in 1842 and then eventually put into service in the War between the States. They were part of Confederate arms at Palmito Ranch, the last battle of the war.

And, finally, we arrive at the mystery.

Some say the guns were shipped back east after the war. Others, however, say the guns were buried. Confederate forces often buried weapons at the end of the war rather than let them fall into Northern hands.

Rumor has it the Twin Sisters were buried in Harrisburg—that would today be in Houston somewhere around the East Loop and Highway 225. They were reportedly hidden somewhere "near the bayou." But is it true? Were

A monument to the Twin Sisters stands in the San Jacinto battleground, just in front of the old battleship USS Texas. As of this writing, there had been talk that the Battleship Texas would be relocated.

Confederate cannons buried in Harrisburg? If so, were they the Twin Sisters?

If you're running around the east side and come across a pair of cannons bearing the inscription "Greenwood's Eagle Ironworks of Cincinnati," please let us know. This one's been underground knowledge long enough.

These two cannons were donated to the Texan cause by the United States for support in the Texas Revolution. But they were lost in the mists of time, and some say they remain buried in the Houston area.

67 TRAINED ARTISTS

What's with the "Be Someone" sign over Interstate 45?

Some find it inspirational. Others see it as a trashy eyesore. Not since the Gulf "lollipop" sign that once adorned the JPMorgan Chase Tower has such a public work divided the town. But who exactly painted that thing? The city? An art collective? Just some guy? How did they do it and why?

"Be Someone" isn't a commissioned work; it's just illegal graffiti painted on a train bridge owned by Union Pacific. The original artist keeps his real name secret, since he's technically a criminal. He works under the simple sobriquet of "Besomeone" and plies his trade by climbing the bridge and hanging down to paint the block letters with a roller brush. He keeps a partner with him as a lookout, since a train crossing that bridge while he's on it would mean nowhere to go but down.

Houston is full of professional, pedigreed modern artists from fancy schools. But that's not Besomone's scene. He came up as a graffiti artist and wanted the "Be Someone" sign to inspire Houstonians. "I want people to understand that you can do what you want to do if you put yourself to it," the artist told KTRK's Pooja Lodhia in a 2016 interview (during which he wore a disguise), "It sounds cliché but . . . you have to get up and go get it."

People paint over it from time to time. But Besomeone keeps repainting. In fact, other Houstonians sometimes help

Some people love it. Some people hate it. But the "Be Someone" graffiti painted on a Union Pacific Railroad trestle above Interstate 45 has become a Houston landmark.

As of this writing, there is a change.org petition to the City of Houston, the Houston Archaeological and Historical Commission, and the Texas State Historical Commission to make this street art a protected landmark. Right now, 33,024 people have signed, although they should probably be asking the railroad that owns it.

BE SOMEONE SIGN

WHAT Popular Guerrilla Art

WHERE I-45 near downtown

COST Free

PRO TIP If you must take a picture of the "Be Someone" sign, it is 100% a two-person job. Driving near downtown is dangerous enough without messing with your phone or camera.

out. Back in 2017, the Input/Output Digital Lab turned the sign into a light show with projection mapping technology. In April 2019, a group of college students dangled upside down to fix the sign when it had been defaced.

Love it or hate it, though, please continue to Be Someone and stay off that bridge so you don't get hurt.

RECREATIONAL REPLAY

What kind of games did people play five thousand years ago?

When we think of ancient peoples, we typically think about how they lived and worked: the agriculture of Mesopotamia, the building of the pyramids at Giza, or the battles of the Chinese Warring States period. But what did people do for fun? After all, people from the past were people just like us—and they did have a little downtime now and again.

Fortunately, Houstonians can learn all about the ancient games that were played around the world at Archeology Now's annual Ancient Games Tournament. Once a year in January, the group hosts this cool event to help bring the games of the past back to life for today's Houstonians. The "A Games," as they've come to be known, let participants connect with the past by playing board games popular in ancient civilizations far away.

The games played at the tournament include chess (which comes in a surprising number of historical variations), Go, Parcheesi, Backgammon, Senet, checkers, and something called the Royal Game of Ur. Senet is a game originating in ancient Egypt; the object is to get all your pieces off the board, and you roll sticks rather than dice. Many people say that today's game of checkers is a descendant of Ur, with modern versions of the game evolving around the sixteenth century. There are a number of interesting games at the A Games, and even more fascinating histories surrounding them.

The A Games is also a proper tournament, where you'll play strangers to determine a winner. Not everyone wins, but everyone learns. The games are kicked off with a super-interesting lecture by an authority on these pastimes of the past—which is interesting enough to warrant a visit even without all the gameplay.

This Japanese print by the ukiyo-e artist Torii Kiyonaga (1752–1815) portrays a group of children fighting while playing Go, one of the oldest board games in the world. The game's origins are murky but commonly thought to lie in China from three to four thousand years ago.

ACTUAL GAMES OF CIVILIZATION

WHAT Ancient Games Tournament

WHERE Memorial City Mall as of now (venue may change)

COST Varies year to year

PRO TIP Get involved, but don't be hypercompetitive. The true beauty of it is the players' connection to the past.

With many people coming to appreciate being unplugged from their devices, retro board games are now all the rage. And there's nothing more retro than games that have been played for thousands of years.

⁶⁹ SECRET SANCTUARY

Have you been to the hidden bird sanctuary off Memorial Drive?

Any bird lover worth his or her binoculars knows about the Edith L. Moore Nature Sanctuary, an eighteen-acre urban forest tucked away off Memorial Drive near Beltway 8. Yet many Houstonians have never heard of it. For more than forty years, it's been a place of peace and tranquility on Houston's west side.

In the early 1920s, Edith Moore bought a homestead along Rummel Creek in west Houston. At the time, this was seventeen miles outside of town. She lived in an actual log cabin she and her husband built themselves during 1931 and 1932. They moved out there to get away from city life. They had cows, chickens, and pigs—the whole homesteading experience.

Moore donated her land to the Houston Audubon Society in 1975. The city, of course, grew around Moore's land. Today the property is in Memorial's Wilchester area, just across the beltway from City Centre. The only cows you'll see around now are Wagyu steaks grilling on Sundays.

Visitors to the tranquil wildlife preserve can walk a number of trails and spot interesting wild birds including—depending on your timing—woodpeckers, egret, heron,

---

The Edith L. Moore Nature sanctuary is a tiny in-town getaway where people come to watch birds, get lost in nature, and learn about the natural environment. Check out its live bird cam at https://houstonaudubon.org/sanctuaries/edith-moore/bird-camera.html.

This blue jay (Cyanocitta cristata) has had its fill of water from one of the sanctuary's bird baths. The small dome-shaped device in the bath creates little ripples so that the birds can find something to drink more easily.

EDITH L. MOORE NATURE SANCTUARY

WHAT Hidden birdwatching spot on the west side

WHERE 440 Wilchester Blvd.

COST Free

PRO TIP Hit the nearby Wild Birds Unlimited. You can buy many of the feeders in use at the sanctuary at the store, including peanut feeders for the blue jays.

geese, owls, hawks, flycatchers, wrens, thrushes, martins, and warblers. You can just wander around or take a self-guided tour on your phone. There are even organized walks where you can come and nerd out with other birds of a feather. If you can't make it out in person, check out the Bird Cam online.

Moore's old cabin is still there as well. It's undergone a number of improvements over the years, including a major restoration in 2012, but it still sports its original 1930s construction. Some of the accent stone is actually recycled curbside material from downtown Houston. The old homestead's even got a fancy parking lot these days. So get out of traffic and into the bird scene. Ka-kaw! Ka-kaw!

SURROUNDING SURNAMES

Do you know some of the names behind everyday Houston places?

City of Houston

Named after Sam Houston (1793–1863), the first and third President of the Republic of Texas. He led the Texas army on the battlefield during the Texas Revolution, served in the Texas House of Representatives, worked as a U.S. Senator, and was a Texas governor. He's the only man in history to serve as governor of two states: Texas and Tennessee.

Westheimer Boulevard

Named after Mitchell Louis Westheimer, who was born in Baden, Germany in 1831. Westheimer moved to Texas in the 1850s, eventually purchasing a sizeable tract of land known as Westheimer Plantation. His massive plantation house is now the site of Lamar High School. He spoke seven languages, grew a number of successful businesses, and was a leader in Congregation Beth Israel.

Harris County

Harris County, and Harrisburg, were both named after John Richardson Harris (1790–1829). A New Yorker by birth, he was one of Austin's "Old Three Hundred" colonists who came to settle Texas under the Mexican government. Sailing to Texas on his own ship, he received 4,428 acres of land and thrived through a number of business interests.

Allen Parkway

Allen Parkway was named after Augustus Chapman Allen and John Kirby Allen, the two slick New Yorkers who founded and developed the City of Houston. John Kirby

The Lamar name is all around Southeast Texas. Georgia-born Mirabeau Buonaparte Lamar was the vice president of the Republic of Texas under Sam Houston, and then the president of Texas (Houston couldn't run immediately after serving his first term due to term limitations). An erudite and educated man, Lamar was a prolific painter and poet.

had owned a hat store before moving to Texas; his brother was a professor of mathematics and bookkeeper. They quit their steady jobs and set off to Texas to make a fortune in land speculation, and did exactly that.

Kirby Drive

Named after John Henry Kirby (1860–1940), an influential lumber magnate from East Texas who settled in Houston and made a big impact over the years. In a very Ayn Randian way, he had railroads built to remote Texas pine regions for easier logistics and then bought, and scaled, a number of operations. He also started an oil company that's still going today.

Going about our daily lives, we don't often stop to think, "Who were these people whose names are a part of everyday H-Town?" T. C. Jester Boulevard, for example, was named after the Reverend Thomas C. Jester who served as pastor of Baptist Temple, a church in the Heights.

⁷¹ PIPE DREAMS

Have you done a drive-by of the city's most creative pipe yard?

Pipe, flanges, and fittings—the unsung heroes of the industrial world. They're the glue that makes the country's industry and infrastructure possible so that your lights come on, you can put gas in your car, and hospitals are able to do their thing. Still, most people don't find all that industrial stuff interesting to look at. Unless, of course, you see it in the Eclectic Menagerie Park.

At this pipe yard just off Highway 288 and Bellfort, one pipe company offers a showcase of metalwork art, piping, and found material that's become legend around town. Built on extra acreage along the freeway, the park offers up metalwork sculptures of a dinosaur, Snoopy flying an airplane, a giant fishing pole catching a pickup truck, an owl (whose feathers look like they were really hard to make), cows, King Kong, a dragon, and a huge armadillo.

My personal favorite is the giant pipe-made spider that looks like something straight out of *Cloverfield* or *War of the Worlds*.

The park was the vision of Texas Pipe & Supply Chairman Jerry Rubenstein, who kicked it off when he bought an outsized hippo sculpture in El Campo. After that, it was on. A number of the pieces were conceived and executed by local artist Ron Lee (check out his beer tap handles at ronlee.com; they're incredible). He made that super-cool spider, which took about nine months.

The pipe yard covers more than one hundred acres, but the Eclectic Menagerie Park occupies only an edge of it by the road. The thing to remember about visiting is that while people refer to it as a park, it's still a pipe yard on the side of the freeway. You can park on the shoulder; it looks like it's been widened just for onlookers, but just be careful.

This wise but welded owl is just one of many creatures you'll find at the Eclectic Menagerie Park—an unexpected private collection of metal sculpture near the South Loop.

THE METAL IS THE MEDIUM

WHAT Eclectic Menagerie Park

WHERE Northwest corner of 288 & West Belfort

COST Free

PRO TIP Stay off the road, and go early in the summer (there's no shade).

Not everybody gets excited about visiting a pipe yard, but drivers who stumble across the Eclectic Menagerie Park are in for an unexpected collection of metalwork that proves creativity can be found anywhere.

BEAVER BUBBLES

Where is the world's longest automated car wash?

It's not on the company's website. And nobody really talks about it. Yet according to the Guinness Book of World Records, the world's longest automated car wash is the Texas-sized drive-through at the Buc-ee's in Katy. At 255 feet long, the automated car wash pulls your vehicle along on a pulley as multiple attendants help you get the car in straight and keep everything moving.

Once you're in, drivers can just slip the car in neutral and chow down on Beaver Nuggets or homemade jerky while they munch their way through the wash. Twenty-five rolling brushes and seventeen dryers get your car squeaky clean from one end to the other, which takes about five minutes. The wash is just 15 feet shy of being a football field in length and up to sixteen cars can run through it at a time—and that's sixteen Texas cars. It cost more than $3 million to build; that's twice the gross domestic product of the South Pacific island of Tokelau.

Taking a look at the Buc-ee's travel center in Katy, it makes sense that it would sport the world's largest car wash. The place is huge. With 120 fuel pumps, the store seems more like an airport than a store or gas station. That's right, as you're reading this somebody is legit using "Pump 112." In fact, it's so big that you hardly notice the world's

According to the Guinness Book of World Records, the car wash at the Katy Buc-ee's location is the world's longest automated car wash. The record for the most beaver nuggets eaten in one road trip remains up for grabs.

The car wash entrance, before driving around back. Big 18-wheelers aren't allowed on the property. Not shown: a line of vacuum stations that stretches practically to College Station.

CAR WASH AT BUC-EE'S KATY

WHAT World's longest automated car wash

WHERE 27700 Katy Freeway

COST $9 to start, $16 for the works

PRO TIP One of you runs the car through; the others shop.

longest automated car wash when you pull in. You have to look for it (it's in the back).

Arch "Beaver" Aplin III and Don Wasek founded the convenience store chain in 1982. The first Buc-ee's was in Lake Jackson. They focused on making sure the ice was plentiful and the restrooms spotless. Today there are thirty-five locations, each one packed with Lone Star gifts, munchies, and drinks. The 50,000-square-foot Katy store opened in 2017.

UNDERGROUND GRUB

What's the best place in Houston to get poke, pizza, and pulled pork sandwiches at 2:00 a.m.?

Houston's first food hall, the Conservatory Underground Beer Garden & Food Hall, is an underground hideout where you can pick from multiple independent restaurants in one conveniently located spot. As of this writing, visitors to the stylishly appointed basement space can choose between El Burro's barbecue, Arte Pizzeria, Moku Bar Poke & Tempura, the Pho Spot, Treacherous Leches, and more.

On Prairie between Main and Fannin, the Conservatory's the perfect spot for downtown coworkers who can't agree on a place—or for satisfying those after-hours cravings on a weekend. My favorite is actually the donut bread pudding from Treacherous Leches (a punny take on the Mexican *tres leches* dessert). The restaurants come and go, although the turnover isn't very high and many are still the originals. That aspect of it is nice, though, because the experience changes a little from time to time. In fact, if you think your restaurant has what it takes you can apply to be a vendor right on the website.

And did we mention the beer garden? Yep, this Houston secret has an underground beer garden, complete with plants and video games. You'll find sixty beers on tap, each carefully curated by the owners, including a number of local selections by Saint Arnold, Karbach Brewing Company, 8th Wonder Brewery, Spindletap Brewery, and more. Most people love a good patio, but the Conservatory is especially nice on ultra-hot Houston days. When it's August and 100 percent humidity, you can duck downstairs and enjoy a beer garden feel without the heatstroke.

For a bonus secret, did you know that the Conservatory is owned by the same people who own Prohibition Theatre next door? If you haven't caught one of their burlesque

Cool and intimate no matter what the weather outside, the Conservatory is the perfect place to regroup at the end of a night out or meet for a quick downtown lunch.

THE CONSERVATORY

WHAT Eclectic, underground food hall

WHERE 1010 Prairie St.

COST Varies

PRO TIP When you first walk in, you'll hit Treacherous Leches. Try the donut bread pudding.

shows, they're amazing. And since the Conservatory is open until 3:00 a.m. on the weekend, you can catch a show and then slide into the Conservatory for an after-hours drink. See you on the downlow.

This underground eatery is open late—the home of The Pho Spot, Noble Rot Wine Bar, Arte Pizzeria, Treacherous Leches, El Burro & the Bull, and Moku Bar Poke & Tempura.

Who bought a former NBA basketball arena and turned it into a church?

Houstonians of a certain age may remember the days when the Houston Rockets played in a city-owned arena called The Summit off Highway 59 at Buffalo Speedway. For the uninitiated, The Summit was built in 1975 and hosted not only Houston Rockets games but also some of the hottest shows in town. It has sixteen thousand seats.

The Grateful Dead, Eric Clapton, Muddy Waters, the Eagles, ZZ Top, David Bowie, and other legends played the venue. It hosted family shows like Disney on Ice. The Houston Comets played there. The Houston Thunderbears, an arena football team, even played there from 1996 until 2001. Yep, WWE wrestling, too. In 1998, The Summit changed its name to Compaq Center, but much like the Compaq name, it wouldn't live much longer.

In 2003, the doors opened at the Toyota Center downtown. The Rockets moved out. The last concert at Compaq Center was in November 2003: ZZ Top, Los Lobos, and Cross Canadian Ragweed.

Enter Joel Osteen.

Osteen is the pastor of Lakewood Church, the most mega of American megachurches. Each week as many as fifty thousand people show up to hear Joel Osteen do his thing. Fifty thousand! That's basically like the entire population of

The Summit/Compaq Center transitioned to the home of today's Lakewood Church. It has a weekly attendance of more than fifty thousand people. That's a lot of hands to shake.

Lakewood Church, where the Houston Rockets once played when it was the Summit. While the building's size is impressive, the church's media reach is even more so—they even have iPhone and Android apps you can use to watch services.

LAKEWOOD CHURCH

WHAT Arena that's been saved

WHERE 3700 Southwest Freeway

COST Free

PRO TIP Unlike a Metallica concert, free childcare is provided during services.

Galveston showing up at some time during the week. And he needed a place to put them.

The Summit was just sitting there, so Osteen's offer was approved. The church spent 18 months and $95 million renovating the space—there's no telling what Mötley Crüe did in there—and held its first service in 2005. Churchgoers love the space, and Osteen's empire has grown by leaps and bounds ever since.

So there you have it. Lakewood Church is now headquartered where Ozzy Osbourne stopped on his *Ultimate Sin* tour and Metallica hammered renditions of "Master of Puppets." Now it's pretty much just "Shout at the Devil" all the time \m/.

FOREIGN GOODS

Where do H-Town's expats shop for groceries?

Houston attracts people from all over the world. So where are all the secret little spots where foreign nationals shop for groceries when they want a taste of home? Here are a few.

Super H-Mart

H-Mart bills itself as a "Korean tradition made in America." Serving all types of Asian food, this awesome place has everything from kimchi to baked goods. The "H" in H-Mart is short for *han ah reum*, which means "one arm full of groceries."

Afghan Halal Market

Afghan Halal Market on Hillcroft is a local favorite for all kinds of Afghan, Pakistani, and Indian foods. You can buy a whole butchered goat, all kinds of Afghani snacks, tea, spices, fruits, and more.

Makola Marketplace

West Bellfort's Makola Marketplace is popular among natives of Nigeria, Senegal, Ghana, and the rest of West Africa. If you're looking to make red-red, jollof rice, or ogbono, this is your best bet.

Seiwa Market

At this Dairy Ashford–area market you'll find a number of Japanese nationals stocking up on their shopping, picking up everything from their favorite brand of sake or yakisoba noodles to a variety of sashimi.

Phoenicia

This isn't much of a secret but, for those few remaining Houstonians who've never been, Phoenicia's Houston locations offer top-notch Mediterranean food, drinks,

Seiwa opened in August 2016 and has since become a go-to spot for authentic Japanese food and groceries.

and more. The founders were Lebanese and Armenian, and the store has become an H-Town treasure.

Mi Tienda

Owned by H-E-B, this store caters to the Hispanic market (Here Everything's Bueno!). They offer an amazing panadería, pescadería, and carnicería as well as authentic products like Bimbo pan dulce, Yemina pasta, La Costeña, cueritos, and Jumex.

British Isles

The presence of BP means that most Houston grocery stores have been selling PG Tips and Weetabix for decades. But British Isles on Rice Boulevard takes it to the next level, bringing authentic British marmalades, crisps, biscuits, chutneys, and gifts that include, God help us, royal keepsakes.

There are eighty foreign consulates in Houston, and that means a lot of expatriates. It also means a lot of awesomely authentic foreign foods around town—if you know where to look.

'80S ACTION

Where were Houston's most notable '80s movie scenes shot?

The most widely acclaimed H-Town movies filmed in the 1980s were *Terms of Endearment* and *Urban Cowboy*. Go behind the scenes to check out the filming locations for these beloved flicks.

Terms of Endearment

This Academy Award–winning 1983 film takes place partly in Houston, with Jack Nicholson and Shirley MacLaine playing out an autumn romance as neighbors. The two homes from the film are in Avalon. The home of Aurora Greenway is at 3060 Locke Lane and looks virtually as it did in the movie. Garrett Breedlove's house next door, 3068 Locke, was the famous Waldo Mansion, where Garrett splashed around in his backyard pool (now a koi pond). It's been remodeled beyond recognition, but you can do as you please when you pay that much for a house. The scene in which the two go out to a fancy lunch date was filmed at Brennan's at 3300 Smith Street.

Urban Cowboy

Sadly, Gilley's in Pasadena, Texas, closed in 1989 and then burned to the ground. That refinery in which John Travolta filmed the scene where he nearly falls is now a Valero, and still there—although the tower he was climbing has since been removed. The home of Bud's Uncle Bob and Aunt

Texas doesn't throw tax credits at Hollywood the way Louisiana does, but we still have a few movie credits to our name. These two are some of the best from the 1980s.

It's been more than thirty years since the release of Terms of Endearment, *and people still request the table at Brennan's where Jack Nicholson and Shirley MacLaine lunched during their date.*

Corrine is 2213 Westside Drive in Deer Park. The fancy apartment Bud's wealthy girlfriend lived in was at 2016 Main, and the club they went to was the Elan at 1885 St. James Place (where an apartment building now stands). The scenes of Bud and Sissy's trailer were filmed in California; you can see mountains in the distance.

Houstonians can actually submit their home, business, or land to the Texas Film Commission as a potential film location, and crews will reach out if they want to use your space.

Other notable films with H-Town scenes: *Reality Bites, Rush, Pearl Harbor, Twins, Tin Cup, Armageddon, Rushmore, Arlington Road, Apollo 13* (though not the Mission Control scenes), *Friday Night Lights, Hellfighters, Amarillo by Morning, Jason's Lyric, RoboCop 2,* and the cult ninja film *Pray for Death.*

77 LUV YA BLUES

Where's the love for Houston's blues music heritage?

New Orleans is known for jazz. Nashville is known for country. Austin is known for outsized music festivals attended by trust fund slackers who ride there on Lime scooters eating whiskey-infused bacon or whatever. But Houston deserves its share of music love, too. And I'm not just talking about the rap or R&B scenes, which do get plenty of well-deserved recognition. I'm talking about Houston blues.

Many people don't know that Houston is one of America's great blues music capitals. Third, Fourth, and Fifth wards all had brilliant blues artists by the 1920s, including the legendary Sam "Lightnin'" Hopkins. Hopkins made his own guitar out of a cigar box and chicken wire at the age of eight. He played with his cousin, Texas Alexander, in the Third Ward and honed his skills until he grew to be a blues legend who made Houston his home. Eventually he was opening for rock bands like the Grateful Dead and giving command performances for the likes of Queen Elizabeth II.

Hopkins recorded more than thirty songs at a local studio called Sugar Hill Recording Studios—which is still very much alive and thriving today. Founded in 1941 by producer Bill Quinn, today's Sugar Hill (originally operating under the names "Quinn" and "Gold Star") recorded an army of blues talent such as Melvin "Lil' Son" Jackson, the "Silver Fox of the Blues" Buddy Ace, and Wilson "Thunder" Smith. Don Robey's Peacock Records and the old Peacock Club brought even more talent.

Evidence of Houston's blues heritage is around if you know what to look for. There's even a traveling exhibit called the Houston Blues Museum that showcases a lot of cool memorabilia. The Big Easy Social and Pleasure Club on Kirby

Hit The Big Easy Social and Pleasure Club over by Rice University for a variety of blues acts—many for free or for just a $5 cover. Bonus lagniappe: Zydeco acts, too.

GOOD AT FEELIN' BAD

WHAT Houston's Blues Heritage

WHERE All over town

COST The despair inherent in the human condition

PRO TIP Don't miss KPFT's Sunday Blues Bruch with Nuri Nuri.

hosts heartbreaking blues. And every Sunday on 90.1 KPFT, Nuri Nuri, the "Big Bad Bossman of the Blues," hosts a Blues Brunch show.

> "So I went ahead and made me a guitar. I got me a cigar box, I cut me a round hole in the middle of it, take me a little piece of plank, nailed it onto that cigar box, and I got me some screen wire and I made me a bridge back there and raised it up high enough that it would sound inside that little box, and got me a tune out of it. I kept my tune and I played from then on."
> —Lightnin' Hopkins

FINE LINES

Hey, what happened to Houston's original electric trains?

From the 1890s until 1940, electric streetcars were *the* way Houstonians traveled around the city. Houston's first streetcars were post–Civil War mule-powered affairs. By 1927, there were sleek electric railcars. That year, ninety miles of track crisscrossed the Bayou City with more than forty-one million rail passengers recorded. Known for most of its life as the Houston Electric Company, the system enabled Houston to spread out and grow in all directions.

So what happened? How did we go from almost one hundred miles of track way back then to struggling for decades to build out today's underwhelming light rail system?

Some will tell you that the death of the streetcar system across the United States is down to a conspiracy by General Motors to buy rail lines and systematically shut them down in cities all across the United States to create a market for the automobile. Who knows—the rest of the country has its own secrets. In Houston, the official story of the original rail lines' demise and the rise of the bus system came mainly down to budget.

The Great Depression hit ridership hard. No job meant no need to catch a railcar. In addition, when a new route was needed, a bus was much cheaper to add than a rail line. The City of Houston kept demanding that the railcar owner and operator, Houston Electric Company, share roadway paving costs. Maintenance costs were high.

But the nail in the coffin was the rise of the automobile. Although World War II put a dent in production, cars were becoming more popular—and more fun. Ford introduced the V8 engine. Drive-in restaurants with carhops opened.

One of today's MetroRail cars takes a break beneath Interstate 45.

The middle class was using automobiles as a means of self-expression. In 1940, Mayor Oscar Holcomb and the Houston Electric Company finally agreed to call it quits on the railcar program. It wasn't until 2001 that limited light rail operations began again.

DERAILED

WHAT Houston's original rail lines

WHERE Gone but not forgotten

COST Road rage

PRO TIP During the Houston Livestock Show and Rodeo, MetroRail gives Houstonians multiple options to park remotely and take the train in.

At one point, Houston had electric railcar lines all over town (granted, it was a smaller town back then). But the city's light rail system was abandoned and completely extinct by the time World War II rolled around.

79 DANG, Y'ALL

Who is H-Town's jeweler to the hip hop stars?

When you see a rapper wearing $100,000 in ostentatious jewelry, have you ever wondered where, exactly, that person bought such a thing? The gold rope chains. The bold diamond encrusted watches. The gold and diamond-encrusted teeth known as "grills." For some of the biggest names in hip hop, the answer is Houston's own Johnny Dang.

If you're plugged into the hip hop scene, you know the name. But for the rest of us, Dang is the behind-the-scenes face of a national jewelry empire. Dang's jewelry is worn by the rap industry's A-list, stars who can sink hundreds of thousands of dollars into custom jewelry.

His business, Johnny Dang & Co., doesn't just sell jewelry—he's an actual manufacturer. Regular folks like us can buy nice pieces at regular prices, but that's not what he's known for. He's known for the bling: thick rope chains and elaborate pendants, diamond earrings, iced-out sunglasses, and custom jewelry of all kinds. When the trend of getting "grills" became a thing, he made them for stars such as Rick Ross, Snoop Dogg, and Travis Scott. Dang's store is where Two Chains gets a lot of his "two chains."

Johnny Dang's father was a jeweler, as was his father before him. The son of one of Houston's many boat people of Vietnam, Dang came to H-Town in 1996 and did what his

HIP HOP'S KING OF BLING

WHAT Johnny Dang & Co.

WHERE 6224 Richmond Ave.

COST How much you got?

PRO TIP You can buy online, assuming your credit card goes up to $180,000.

Johnny Dang & Co is on Richmond Avenue just outside Loop 610. You might have heard of his business partner, rapper Paul Wall. Dang has more than fifty people on staff.

family had always done best—make jewelry. He started small at the swap meet and then gradually grew his business. Today he's known among the hip hop crowd as the "King of Bling"—a true American success story.

To my mind, one of his coolest pieces involves a different kind of monster star. In May 2019, he partnered with Warner Brothers to make a special one-of-a-kind diamond Godzilla chain and pendant encrusted with diamonds, rubies, and emeralds. The price? If you have to ask, you can't afford it.

Dang told the *Houston Chronicle* recently that his shop makes twenty to thirty custom pieces each week, setting between fifteen and twenty thousand diamonds along the way. That's a lot of bling.

80

NEWBIE TRANSLATIONS

What are some H-Town Terms a newcomer might not know?

Astrodomain

This complex of properties once included the Astrodome, a nearby hotel, and the now defunct AstroWorld amusement park—which is today just a place to park during the rodeo.

Bey

Bey is the nickname for Houston's own Beyoncé Giselle Knowles-Carter, the legendary singer-songwriter who has sold more than 100 million records and won twenty-three Grammy awards. Fun fact: Beyoncé fans are known collectively as the "Beyhive."

Houstonia

Houstonia is H-Town's premier news, lifestyle, and entertainment magazine. This SagaCity publication is run from the Heights; it was founded in 2013.

Katy Freeway

Interstate 10 going westbound toward the suburb of Katy is known as the *Katy Freeway*. The same eastbound stretch of highway is referred to as the *East Freeway or Baytown Freeway*.

Nutcracker

No, it's not a pothole reference; the Nutcracker is actually a huge Christmas market put on by the Houston Ballet, coinciding with the ballet's production of *The Nutcracker* each year.

Today's Fertitta Center is the home of Houston Cougar basketball. Back when Phi Slama Jama, "the world's tallest fraternity," played there, the stadium was known as the Hofheinz Pavilion. Their coach was Guy Lewis, himself a UH grad (class of 1947).

Pancho Claus

This Santa Claus–like character is portrayed by Richard Reyes each year as he hops into a low rider and distributes Christmas gifts to disadvantaged kids in Hispanic Houston neighborhoods.

Phi Slama Jama

Phi Slama Jama is a reference to the men's college basketball team at the University of Houston between 1982 and 1984. Playing for the Coogs that year were greats such as Clyde Drexler and Hakeem Olajuwon.

Slab Cars & Swangas

A slab is an American luxury car that is "Slow, Loud, and Bangin'" with candy paint, protruding Swanga wire wheels, and music so loud it will clear your sinuses in April.

"Slime in the Ice Machine!"

The catchphrase of the late Marvin Zindler (1921–2007), a prominent investigative journalist. In his later years, Zindler made famous a news report outing restaurants with health violations. He was so hard-core that he even reported the coffee shop in his own television station.

Trill

A portmanteau of true and real. That's what you should be keeping it, FYI.

81

THE BUTLER DID IT

Why was Rice University's namesake murdered?

Born in Massachusetts in 1816, William Marsh Rice moved to Texas in the late 1830s when it was still an independent country. He rolled into town with nothing, taking a job as a hotel bartender. But Houston was new, founded just that year, and opportunity abounded. By 1840, he was a landowner and merchant. Soon he became what was known as a "cotton factor," providing brokerage and banking services to plantations.

He soon amassed a fortune, leveraging his commercial acumen into an empire that included everything from shipping to insurance. By the 1880s, he had millions and he wanted to give back. He established an endowment in 1891 for a private polytechnic school.

Rice moved to New York in later years, as a means to protect his assets from a dodgy will set up by his ex-wife's family. But eventually one of the lawyers he'd hired to protect his assets from money-grubbing family members began conspiring with Rice's butler to poison the old man and steal the fortune himself. At first, the pair tried poisoning him with mercury. But Rice fought through it. Finally, they succeeded in killing him with chloroform on September 23, 1900.

The lawyer had forged a number of documents that would enable him to secure the Rice fortune. But, like most criminals, he wasn't nearly as smart as he thought. When he tried writing himself a series of checks totaling $250,000—the day after Rice's murder—people back in Houston got suspicious. The lawyer and the butler were both imprisoned.

The Rice Institute opened in 1912. William Marsh Rice's ashes were buried below a statue of him on campus. The initial endowment was so large that it not only allowed

This statue of William Marsh Rice, created by John Angel, sits in the campus quadrangle at Rice and contains the founder's ashes. The students refer to him as "Willie" and once turned the statue completely around as a prank (it literally weighs a ton).

DEATH OF PATRON

WHAT William Marsh Rice Statue and Gravesite

WHERE 6100 Main St.

COST Free

PRO TIP Keep an eye on your butler.

for the financing of the school's construction, startup, and operation, but also enabled every single student to attend the university free of tuition from the school's opening until 1965.

The men who conspired to murder William Marsh Rice got outrageously light sentences, although they didn't go on to live happily ever after. Mr. Patrick, the attorney, was sentenced to death, spending four years on death row at Sing Sing Correctional Facility before eventually being given a pardon. But he lived in Oklahoma, so there's punishment of a sort. Jones, the butler, was set free but committed suicide in Baytown.

82

SAY "CHEESE"

When is the last time you visited a real-life cheesemonger?

Ever wonder where your favorite restaurants in Houston get their finest cheeses? Chances are, if they really know their stuff, they buy from Houston Dairymaids. Originally an exclusive cheese wholesaler, Houston Dairymaids supplies artisan cheese to some of the best restaurants in town. And, luckily for Houstonians everywhere, founder Lindsey Schechter threw open the doors to her store on Airline Drive in 2012 so she could offer her gourmet selection to everyone.

Selling to the public out of a charming old building from the 1930s, Houston Dairymaids curates natural, hand-made cheeses from across the country and Texas, bringing them to dinner tables and restaurants around town. Unless your taste runs to the extremely obscure, there likely isn't a type of cheese you want that you can't find here.

Visitors to the store get a guided cheese tasting that features six different cheeses each week. They go out of their way to promote Texas cheesemakers, such as the Redneck Cheddar (which contains Shiner beer) from the Veldhuizen Family Farm or goat Gouda from Latte Da Dairy. They also sell things that go well with a fine cheese, such as cured meats, olives, honey, and a carefully selected variety of wines and beers—not to mention massive artisan cheese trays and even a cheese-of-the-month club.

Houston Dairymaids also frequently has cheese tastings at various restaurants and breweries around town—including classes that can make you a true cheese expert.

Much like the greengrocer and the haberdashery, cheesemongers in the United States have in large part fallen by the wayside. Big box stores selling pounds of cheese

HOUSTON DAIRYMAIDS

WHAT Good, old-fashioned cheesemonger

WHERE 2201 Airline Dr.

COST Varies by cheese

PRO TIP Hit Wino Wednesdays.

Houston Dairymaids has an amazing selection of cheese. Their cheesemongers can make the perfect picks for any occasion—and make sure you'll have enough for everyone. Even if that occasion is just a nice bottle of wine and Netflix. Photo courtesy of Houston Dairymaids.

from overseas, grocery store delis, and the trend of people sometimes caring less about what they eat have made it a rare calling. But thanks to Houston Dairymaids, the tradition of the cheesemonger is aging nicely indeed.

The Cheese-of-the-Month Club sounds kind of, well, cheesy, but after tasting some of what's on offer, the *Secret Houston* team approves. Those on the receiving end get three handmade cheeses each month, each so good you'll be on the wedge of your seat waiting for the next delivery.

83

STORAGE TOURS

Where does the Houston Museum of Natural Science keep its offsite treasures?

Since 1909, the Houston Museum of Natural Science has been an important Houston cultural centerpiece. It houses permanent exhibits that include a gem vault, the Weiss Energy Hall, Fabergé eggs, a hall of ancient Egyptian artifacts, and more, not to mention the many rotating exhibitions, Wortham Giant Screen Theatre, and planetarium. From prehistoric beasts to exhibits presenting the chemistry of the Big Bang, millions of visitors from across the globe experience the natural world through the museum each year.

Few people know about, much less get to see, the secret off-site location in which the museum stores its treasures. In a three-story Montrose building whose exact location is not widely publicized, the museum stores millions of natural artifacts. It's a phenomenal sight—crammed stem-to-stern with Amazonian shrunken heads, tons of intricate taxidermy (including a giant African elephant), dinosaur bones, pottery, Native American artifacts, seashells, bug and butterfly collections, retro technologies, and rare photography.

Less than 10 percent of the museum's artifacts are on display at any given time, according to museum officials. That means whatever you can't see in the spotlight is kept here, and the facility is more than just a dusty garage. The museum is constantly acquiring new materials and rotating works on display. So at any given time, staff members and volunteers are hard at work around the place unpacking, packing, cataloguing, and making sure that everything stays safe, secure, and organized.

Once a quarter, HMNS staff members conduct an exclusive tour of this fascinating off-site storage facility with

The Houston Museum of Natural Science holds sixteen permanent exhibits, each with hundreds, if not thousands, of pieces. There are 100+ marine trilobites alone and hundreds of minerals. Only a small fraction of these works are on display at the actual museum.

HOUSTON MUSEUM OF NATURAL SCIENCE

WHAT HMNS Offsite Collections Storage Tours

WHERE 5555 Hermann Park Dr.

COST $75; $55 for HMNS Members

PRO TIP Book early because it fills up fast.

a limited number of people. Participants meet at the museum and are then transported to the undisclosed location. As of this writing, tickets are $75 ($55 for HMNS members), and the next scheduled tour is sold out more than a month in advance. The only way to see this secret spot is to wait for the next available tour date and snag some tickets.

Each quarter, the Houston Museum of Natural Science gives a guided tour of the museum's offsite storage facility—a behind-the-scenes glimpse of this mind-blowing and eclectic assortment of artifacts and curiosities.

84

FILM AL FRESCO

Where can you go to catch a rooftop movie—and pick up groceries?

As the sun begins to set uptown, the traffic at BLVD Place on San Felipe and Post Oak whizzes by as people go about their daily lives. Above the hustle and bustle of it all, a lucky group of Houstonians is sipping cocktails and watching the sunset as they're waiting for their movie to start. It's the Rooftop Cinema Club—Houston's first rooftop movie theater.

A concept first launched in 2011 on a London rooftop, Houston's Rooftop Cinema Club screens iconic and themed movies—yep, you guessed it—on a rooftop surrounded by a glittering cityscape. The audience lounges in comfy deck chairs or love seats. Wireless headphones ensure that you don't miss anything because of the passing airplanes or sirens, and they even have blankets to help you get all snuggly.

They don't just screen the latest blockbusters; it's more about all-time favorites—*Dirty Dancing, E.T., Weird Science, 9 to 5,* and *Romy and Michele's High School Reunion.* There are even sing-alongs to pics like *Grease, Bohemian Rhapsody,* and *The Greatest Showman.*

Rooftop Cinema Club serves up awesome munchies, too, including bottomless popcorn and gourmet hotdogs by Good Dog Houston. Before the film, people gather to watch the sunset or just catch up. The full bar includes craft beers

The big corporate cineplex at the mall is for suckers. Ditch the cookie-cutter experience for a boutique rooftop cult classic at the Rooftop Cinema Club.

People start gathering well in advance of the movie to have a drink, chat, and unwind. The breeze on the rooftop feels great, and if it gets too chilly, they even have blankets you can use.

ROOFTOP CINEMA CLUB

WHAT Unique cult movie film space

WHERE 1700 Post Oak Blvd.

COST Lawn chairs start at $17

PRO TIP Book well in advance.

and cinema-themed cocktails, such as the Citizen Sugar Cane and The Hills Have Ryes. A quick intermission is held during the film, so everyone can reload or have a smoke.

And—added bonus—this roof we've been talking about? It's actually the roof of a Whole Foods Market. You can grab some free-trade, locally sourced, organic vegan kale mist or whatever. In fact, it's in a complex called BLVD Place that includes other cool spots such as a luxury apartment complex, True Food Kitchen, Sozo Sushi, Luxington, and Bellami. See you up top!

85

NAKED AND UNAFRAID

Is there really a Houston-area lake that lets you sun it all?

Fishing. Sailing. Camping. Lots of people enjoy a day at the lake. And, as it turns out, some people enjoy it even more if they don't have to pack their swimsuit. That's where Emerald Lake Resort comes in.

About thirty minutes north of Houston in Porter, Texas, Emerald Lake is the Houston area's premier nudist resort—where you can enjoy a classic day at the lake, only completely sans clothing. Whereas taking your top off at Lake Conroe could possibly result in a SWAT team deployment, Emerald Lake is skinny dipping central. Houstonians in their birthday suits swim, kayak, play water volleyball and more—all in their natural state.

Emerald Lake Resort is a family place with a family vibe. There are kids running around, and plenty of retirees. There's no hanky-panky happening out in the open; in fact, that sort of thing will get you kicked out posthaste. So will gawking at someone, making people feel weird, or bringing in a handgun (good luck with that concealed carry). It's just a bunch of nature-loving nudists letting it all hang out in the sunshine.

And apparently you have to let it all hang out if you want to hang out at all. Nudity is mandatory at Emerald Lake Resort. So don't just swing by to get rid of your tan lines for a few minutes. Bring enough sunscreen to last the whole stay.

Visitors drive in their RVs, camp in tents, or rent cabins. Many campers are avid birdwatchers, and there is reportedly a pair of mating bald eagles at the lake. There's an outdoor heated spa, a gym, and boat rentals. There's even an island in the middle of the lake and a driving range

With scenes like this, it's no wonder so many people head up to this lake in search of getting back to nature au naturale. The lake has an actual island and, best of all, there's no place to keep your smartphone. Photo courtesy of Emerald Lake Naturist Resort and RV Park.

EMERALD LAKE NATURIST RESORT

WHAT No-clothes lake hideaway

WHERE 23198 TX-494 Loop in Porter

COST $30 day pass

PRO TIP Wear sunscreen.

(bring your own, er, balls). So if living free is your cup of tea, trek out to Emerald Lake Resort and get natural. Just don't forget the bug spray.

Just south of New Caney, Emerald Lake is one of eight nudist resorts scattered around Texas like bathing suits on a summer lawn. It's the only one in the Houston area.

86

WING STOP

Where can you take a walk surrounded by butterflies?

Ever wonder what that weird-looking, cylindrical, tinted building attached to the side of the Houston Museum of Natural Science is? From the outside, this odd-looking structure doesn't look like much. But inside this multimillion-dollar complex is a lush, carefully engineered environment filled with thousands of butterflies imported from all over the world. It's the Cockrell Butterfly Center—where you can take a walk into the rainforest right from the heart of the museum district.

The three-story glass building is an intricate rainforest conservatory centered around a fifty-foot waterfall. It's filled with exotic living plants and kept at optimal conditions as a butterfly environment. Hundreds of species of butterflies fly around inside this giant pod of beautiful plants and flowers, eating nectar and fluttering around the place. And you can just walk in and hang out in it all. There's even an identification guide that lets you get to know your butterflies on the way in.

The Cockrell Butterfly Center gets thousands of new butterflies shipped to it each week from Africa, Asia, and Central and South America. You'll see more than a thousand live butterflies at once in the Cockrell's rainforest conservatory, including all kinds of butterfly-like creatures that include the praying mantis, the giant long-legged

---

This strange-looking building attached to the Houston Museum of Natural Science contains a hidden world of butterflies and other bugs—all nestled into a living habitat. It's so relaxing in there that you kind of just want to hang out and read a book or something.

COCKRELL BUTTERFLY CENTER

WHAT Walk-in rainforest habitat

WHERE 5555 Hermann Park Dr.

COST $12 for adults

PRO TIP Keep the experience going by planting a butterfly garden at home.

Officials at the butterfly center say you can expect to see about fifty different species of butterfly when you walk around inside the facility. But there will be more than 1,000 butterflies fluttering around in there with you. Photo courtesy of the Houston Museum of Natural Science.

katydid, the whipscorpion, and the giant prickly stick (which pretty much looks as advertised).

The rainforest conservatory is the big sexy bit, but don't forget to hit the Brown Hall of Entomology while you're there. This multilevel space gives you all kinds of insect insights in the form of models, real-life specimens, interactive exhibits, and more. Be sure to check out both the Chrysalis Corner, where you can see butterflies bust out of their cocoons and spread their wings for the first time, and the Insect Vending Machine, where you can get actual edible bugs!

87

LOCALLY SOURCED WELCOME

Did you know Houston visitors can get a local to tell them all about the city?

Not many people know this, but people who are new to town can book time with a local greeter who'll show them around and tell them all about Houston. The program is part of a nonprofit organization called Houston Greeters, and hundreds of visitors to H-Town have used it to connect with Houstonians who want to share some insights into the nation's fourth-largest city.

People who are interested can just go to the website houstongreeters.org and choose a category they'd like to learn more about: Arts & Culture, Houston Institutions, Local Food & Beverage, etc. Next, just choose a "greet" from the list (a map is included). You can choose different times and languages for your greeter. Finally, your greeter meets you for the insider's experience to whatever you're doing.

It's a bit like Uber, only rather than a ride you're getting a few hours exploring something specific about Houston. And unlike Uber, it's absolutely free. It's not limited to just newcomers, either; people who live here also take the volunteers up on their gratis adventure.

Greeters are all volunteers. Anyone can become a greeter, assuming you follow the group's rules and principles. Typically, these are just people who are super enthusiastic about Houston in general, certain things to do in Houston,

Greeters are all volunteers. You can sign up to create a greet of your own on the Houston Greeters website.

HOUSTON GREETERS

WHAT Warm welcomes and new experiences

WHERE All around town

COST Free

PRO TIP Greets change, so keep checking back at houstongreeters.org.

Coco here is an official Houston Greeter, typically accompanied by Adrienne and Andrew, who host a greet called Coffee + Dogs at Buffalo Bayou. You can bring your own dogs to the greet, which starts at The Dunlavy, goes along the bayou to Johnny Steele Dog Park, and finds its way back to The Dunlavy for a relaxing cup of coffee. Photo courtesy of Adrienne Saxe.

or just sharing local experiences. Generally greeters aren't "Newstonians," but they have lived here for a while and speak a variety of languages.

The program was modeled after similar programs in New York and Chicago. Depending on what volunteer greeters want to show visitors, the greets change from time to time. As of this writing, current greets include things like Coffee + Dogs at Buffalo Bayou, Live Gulf Coast Blues, A Stroll Around Montrose, A Walking Tour Around Rice University, and many more.

88

THE DEATH AND DIAMONDS TOUR

Money doesn't always buy happiness; sometimes it buys murder.

The verdant neighborhood of River Oaks is one of Houston's most prestigious addresses. From the elaborate holiday decorations to the phalanx of charity dinners, it is the official residence of Houston's great and good. But now Houstonians can take a true crime tour of the neighborhood and get the juice on the crimes behind that immaculate landscaping.

Veteran tour guide Vicki Clakley takes guests on a private car tour of the River Oaks neighborhood in which she gives you the goods on five or six different murders of prominent River Oaks residents. She drives you by the houses and gives you all the sordid stories surrounding these cases, which were big news at the time but have faded in the age of the twenty-four-hour news cycle.

The cases she covers include the scandalous case of Dr. John Hill and Joan Robinson Hill. John Hill was a world-famous plastic surgeon, and his wife was the prominent daughter of Texas oilman Ash Robinson. He was also a cheater who chose to personally drive his wife to an oddly distant hospital when she mysteriously fell ill in 1969.

Storyteller and professional tour guide Vicki Clakley is a native Texan who offers a true crime tour of the tony River Oaks neighborhood. She knows where all the bodies are buried, so to speak. Request a tour at historygurl.vc@gmail.com.

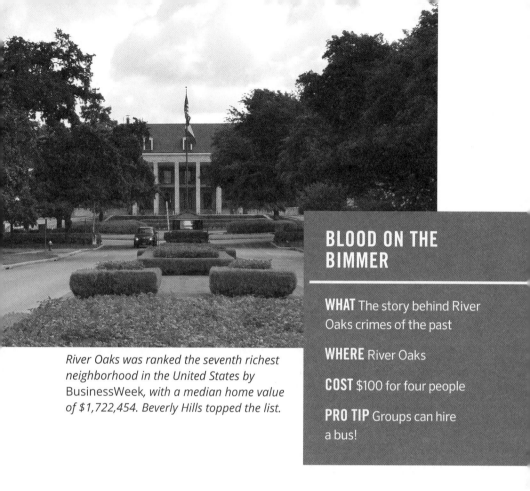

River Oaks was ranked the seventh richest neighborhood in the United States by BusinessWeek, with a median home value of $1,722,454. Beverly Hills topped the list.

BLOOD ON THE BIMMER

WHAT The story behind River Oaks crimes of the past

WHERE River Oaks

COST $100 for four people

PRO TIP Groups can hire a bus!

She died. He immediately married his lover, Ann Kurth, who ended up testifying against Hill when he was tried for his wife's murder. The case, however, ended in a mistrial.

They say what goes around comes around, but it comes around much more quickly when a wealthy Houston oilman thinks you killed his daughter. Hill was set to be retried for the crime, but before the trial he answered his front door one day and was shot dead on the doorstep of his River Oaks mansion. Ash Robinson retired to Florida.

The case was the subject of numerous books and movies, including the made-for-TV movie *Murder in Texas* starring Sam Elliot, Farrah Fawcett, and Andy Griffith. It's just one of Clakley's stops on her "Death and Diamonds" tour.

So you know the Art Car Parade. But have you been to the Art Car Museum?

Houston has no shortage of art galleries and museums. From the leviathan-like Museum of Fine Arts, Houston to the sprawling complexes of the Washington Avenue Arts District and its 300+ studios, it's tough to make time for it all. But one of the most interesting experiences is exploring some of Houston's smaller art spaces. Case in point: the Art Car Museum.

This quirky and carefully curated contemporary art museum is meant to give voice to art cars and other artists who might not otherwise get consideration from the usual art scene. Its goal is to "encourage the public's awareness of the cultural, political, economic and personal dimensions of art."

The automobile, especially here in the states, is often seen as an expression of individualism. The museum's vehicles are intentional and extreme expressions of this car-as-personal-statement. It's a medium that can be strikingly high-concept when done well, and when people stop to give these works true consideration.

One thing that surprises many visitors is the quality and variety of non-wheeled art on display. The modestly sized space is positively rich with everything from multimedia installations to sculpture to pen-and-pencil work. When the

---

This quirky and carefully curated museum is dedicated to the motor vehicle as artistic medium, but it also offers a number of distinctive and impactful artwork of the non-wheeled variety.

As with all art museums and galleries, many specific works on display come and go. You're looking at an art car tribute to Stevie Ray Vaughn created by kids in the Houston Heights High School art program, under the direction of Rebecca Bass.

CREATIVITY WITH MOMENTUM

WHAT Art Car Museum

WHERE 140 Heights Blvd.

COST Free

PRO TIP Park next door at the Citgo station, and your car will be crushed and melted within five minutes and possibly transformed into an art installation exploring the cost of nonconformity.

Secret Houston team visited, the work of the old school Lawndale set was on display—showcasing a diverse and heavy-hitting collection that was every bit as powerful as you'd expect from that crowd. But the place is always mixing it up, with fresh exhibits and events. So it's not the kind of place you just visit and forget about.

The Art Car Museum has its roots in a 1984 show at the original Lawndale Art Center called Collision, curated by prominent Houston artist Ann Harithas. The show featured California's Larry Fuente and his "Mad Cad" 1960 Cadillac adored with jewels, beads, ducks, and female mannequin bits. H-Town loved it, and the appreciation snowballed into a passionate Houston art car movement.

What happens when four comedians pull together to start a comedy venue?

At the corner of Polk and St. Emanuel Streets, painted all black, you'll find one of Houston's funkiest comedy and music venues. With an underground speakeasy vibe, this high-energy collaboration is helping Houstonians discover the massive groundswell of creative talent on tap here in H-Town.

The Secret Group was started by comedians Reed Marshal Becker, Stephen Brandau, Andrew Youngblood, and Jack Watkins Jr. Its founders may be driven entrepreneurs, but they were comics and creatives first who had a vision of bringing something new to town. The scrappy group did whatever it took to make their vision a reality, including a GoFundMe page that lets you donate money to the club in exchange for having a toilet stall named after you (insert revenue stream joke here). The result was a vibrant and distinctive scene that's become irreplaceable in just a few years.

Every night is something new. Speedball: three-minute open-mic comedy sets. Bowl Cuts: the roast of filmmakers' early works. Lady Bits: Houston's funniest women. Dance parties. The One-Off Pun Off contest. There's real magic every night, and many Houstonians have no idea. When the *Secret Houston* team visited, the club was hosting a live broadcasting of the Tin Foil Hat Comedy podcast, a funny conspiracy-themed podcast with Sam Tripoli and special guest Eddie Bravo.

The place is also a steal, moneywise. Unlike most clubs, there isn't a drink minimum. There's a two-dollar well night. Some nights they have free pizza (good pizza) or free chips and salsa. They have "pay what you can" shows, and parking

The Secret Group even has a rooftop patio. Each month they host Bad Idea: A Pay-What-You-Can Comedy Show hosted by Zahid Dewji with free pizza from Russo's.

THE SECRET GROUP

WHAT Indie comedy powerhouse

WHERE 2101 Polk St.

COST Depends on the night or act. Often free, $5, or pay-what-you-can.

PRO TIP This isn't Costco; don't expect to just roll up and park. You may have to work a little to find a spot, especially if there's a Dynamo or 'Stros game. Park in the bike lane on Polk Street and the joke will be on you.

is reasonable, especially given how hot that part of town has become. The place is also right by some other cool nightspots, such as 8th Wonder Brewery, Miss Carousel, the Truck Yard, and Chapman and Kirby—so you can hit that part of town early and work your way up to a show.

Not everyone in town knows The Secret Group, but nationwide the independent club's creative drive is upping Houston's street cred for comedy.

SOURCES

1. **Knock, Knock**
   Management discussion, April, 2019; https://www.lastconcert.com; https://houstorian.wordpress.com/2007/04/15/last-concert-cafe; Parks, L.B., "A good cafe is hard to find," *Houston Chronicle*, September 17, 1988; "Knock, Knock: Houston's There," by Catherine Matusow, *Houstonia*, October 24, 2016; "Always a classic, Last Concert Café is now a historic landmark: Former speakeasy gets protected status," by Sarah Rufca, *Culture Map Houston,* July 12, 2011; personal discussion with manager.

2. **Beast Mode**
   https://www.shrp.com; Camel and Ostrich Racing, https://www.shrp.com/events/detail/live-thoroughbred-racing-53; "Ostriches, Camels, and Arabians: SHRP Hosts the Amethyst Jewel in Houston," *Houston Press* by Susie Tommaney, February 22, 2018; "Wiener Dog Races at Sam Houston Race Park Saturday," *Houston Chronicle*, February 7, 2012; PHOTOS: Wiener dog races at Sam Houston Race Park, ABC13, February 21, 2016.

3. **Seriously Wilde Shopping**
   https://www.wildecollection.com/; "The Wilde Collection," *Atlas Obscura*; "Wilde Collection Is Houston's Newest and Creepiest Shop," *Houston Press,* October 1, 2015, "The Addams Family Comes to Houston: Discover the Wilde Collection," *Houstonia,* Sarah Rufca Nielsen, 10/12/2015; "Rogue taxidermy, 'haunted' pieces make this Heights shop Wilde," *Houston Chronicle*, Marcy de Luna, April 23, 2019.

4. **Golden Globes**
   "Most Unknown: Ashford Point Palace of the Golden Orbs," *Swamplot*; "Chong Hua Sheng Mu Holy Palace: A Houston Oddity," *Explore Houston with Peggy*, July 25, 2017; "Five of Houston's Weirdest and Wackiest Buildings" by Michael Hardy and John Nova Lomax, *Houstonia*, October 7, 2013; personal visit whereby I almost got mugged by paint huffers.

5. **Life and Death on the Northside**
   https://www.nmfh.org; "The National Museum of Funeral History, hidden in a Houston suburb, is a bizarre, spooky treat" by Marcy de Luna, *Houston Chronicle*, June 24, 2019; "National Museum of Funeral History Gives Glimpse Into Presidential Burials" by Sam Byrd, *Houston Press,* December 2018; "National Museum of Funeral History is heating up with new cremation exhibit" by Craig Hlavaty, *Houston Chronicle*, September 7, 2018; chilling personal visit whereby I vowed to take my cholesterol medicine more regularly.

6. **Secret Asian Land**
   http://www.luckylandhouston.net/; "Lucky Land: Terra-Cotta Army," RoadsideAmerica.com; "New China-inspired park in Houston features Forbidden Garden's old terra-cotta soldiers" by Darla Guillen, *Houston Chronicle*, January 27, 2017; "The strange last days of Forbidden Gardens" by Lisa Gray, *Houston Chronicle*, January 31, 2011; "Chinese Takeout: Texans Buy Up Katy's 'Forbidden' Treasures" by Angel Gonzalez, *Wall Street Journal*, February 22, 2011; personal visit in the rain.

7. **Logan's Run**
   Lost Houston by me; "Camp Logan: Houston, Texas 1917–1919" by Louis F. Aulbach, Linda C. Gorski, et al., April 24, 2014, Handbook of Texas Online, Claudia Hazlewood, "CAMP LOGAN," accessed July 14, 2019, http://www.tshaonline.org/handbook/online/articles/qcc26. Personal visit; searched for camp remains at driving range while drinking beer.

8. **Ghosts in Gray**
   Handbook of Texas Online, Margaret Hopkins Edwards, rev. by R. Matt Abigail, "ADDICKS, TX," accessed July 14, 2019, http://www.tshaonline.org/handbook/online/articles/hla04; "Houston's haunts extend beyond downtown" by Sarah Rufca, *Houston Chronicle*, October 23, 2013; "Top Haunted Places In Houston," CBS, October 7, 2013; "3 Katy ghost stories to check out this Halloween season" by Emily Lincke, *Houston Chronicle*, October 11, 2017; personal visit but not at night! C'mon, what do you expect for a $20 cover price?

9. **Swayze's Secret Spot**
   Handbook of Texas Online, Kassie Dixon, "SWAYZE, PATRICK WAYNE," accessed July 14, 2019, http://www.tshaonline.org/handbook/online/articles/fsw35; "Oak Forest resident Patrick Swayze, from those who knew him" by Betsy Denson, *The Leader,* August 18, 2015; "Suchu's GOOFy New Strip Center Home is Where Patrick Swayze Learned to Dance," *Swamplot* https://www.biography.com/actor/patrick-swayze; "The Time of His Life" by Eileen Smith, *Texas Monthly,* September 2009; indulgent visit to Myti-Burger.

10. **What the Heck Is a Ward?**
    "When There Were Wards: A Series," *Houston History Magazine,* July 12, 2011; "A System of Government Where Business Ruled" by Betty Trapp Chapman; "Houston's First Ward – Producing Food from Farm to Counter" by Betty Trapp Chapman; "From Das Zweiter to El Segundo, A Brief History of Houston's Second Ward" by Thomas McWhorter; "Third Ward, Steeped in Tradition of Self-reliance and Achievement" by Ezell Wilson; "Sixth Ward: Carving Out Its Own Place" by Janet K. Wagner; "Pride lives on in Houston's six historical wards" by Jeannie Never, *Houston Chronicle*, September 7, 2004; http://firstwardhouston.org/

11. **Parkway to the Past**
    "Grand Parkway project uncovers prehistoric remains" by Matthew Tresaugue, *Houston Chronicle*, July 26, 2012; "Ancient burial site may stall Grand Parkway project" by Matthew Tresaugue, *Houston Chronicle*, October 13, 2012; "Prehistoric human remains found along Hwy 99" by ABC13, July 26, 2012; "Amateur archaeologists sift through dirt from construction site" by Lisa Gray, *Houston Chronicle*, January 18 2014; "The Grand Parkway Ancient Burial Site, Up Close and Personal" by Allyn West, *Swamplot*, January 4, 2013.

12. **Going Down**
    "Hydrogeology and simulation of groundwater flow and land-surface subsidence in the northern part of the Gulf Coast Aquifer System, Texas, 1891-2009," by Kasmarek, Mark C., Geological Survey (U.S.), Harris-Galveston Coastal Subsidence District (Tex.), Fort Bend Subsidence District., Lone Star Groundwater Conservation District (Tex.), Created / Published, Reston, Va : U.S. Dept. of the Interior, U.S. Geological Survey, 2012; "For years, the Houston area has been losing ground" by John D. Harden, *Houston Chronicle*, May 28, 2016; "Gigantic Water Tunnels Won't Save Houston From the Next Harvey" by Eric Holtaus, *CityLab*, April 11, 2018; "New app shows exactly where Houston is sinking" by Dylan Baddour, *Houston Chronicle*, July 20, 2017; "For years, engineers have warned that Houston was a flood disaster in the making. Why didn't somebody do something?" by Ralph Vartabedian, *LA Times,* August 29, 2017.

13. **Secret Rendezvous**
    http://www.marfresshouston.com/; "The mystery lies beyond the door of Marfreless" by Syd Kearney, *Houston Chronicle*, November 16, 2012; "Behind the Blue Door of the Reopened, Renovated Make-Out Bar Marfreless" by Angelica Leicht, *Houston Press,* February 5, 2014; visited, but I do not kiss and tell.

14. **Hidden Gem**
    http://thesecret.pbworks.com/w/page/86302954/Image%2008; "The 35-year-old hunt for Hermann Park's buried treasure continues" by Fernando Ramirez, *Houston Chronicle*, May 16, 2017; "Hidden Houston: A secret treasure in Hermann Park" by ABC13, May 1, 2017; "Buried treasure in Hermann Park?" by Carolina Gonzales, *Houston Chronicle*, November 16, 2015; "The quest to find 12 hidden treasures from a 1982 treasure hunt book," BoingBoing.net, July 15, 2014; maybe I found it and maybe I didn't.

15. **Secret Squeeze**
    https://irmasoriginal.com/; "Liquid Assets" by Patricia Sharpe, *Texas Monthly*, July 2005; *Houston Chronicle* Top 100 Restaurants, 23. Irma's, https://www.houstonchronicle.com/entertainment/top-100-restaurants/article/23-Irma-s-4781816.php; sampled personally.

16. **Secret Cistern**
    https://buffalobayou.org/visit/destination/the-cistern/; "Houston Underground: The Buffalo Bayou Park Cistern" by Marika Flatt and Gabi De la Rosa, *Texas Standard*, November 30, 2017; "A Vintage Cistern by the Bayou in Houston Pairs Art and Infrastructure" by Cynthia Lescalleet, *Forbes*, May 7, 2018.

17. **Skyline Felines**
    "Your Secret Cat Code Has Been Cracked, Mr. Johnson," *Swamplot*, October 9, 2009; "What is at the top of the imposing Williams Tower?" by Craig Hlavaty, *Houston Chronicle*, November 6, 2017.

18. **Bank Vault**
    "Burial crypt in downtown Houston tells part of Houston's history" by ABC13 KTRK, October 24, 2014; "Historic burial vault lies hidden in plain sight under downtown Houston bridge" by Carol Christian, *Houston Chronicle*, November 1, 2014; "Texas Traveler: Houston Haunts" by Brittanie Shey, *Houston Press*, October 26, 2009; "Remains pulled from Bayou crypt in 1901" by Carolina Gonzales, *Houston Chronicle*, December 3, 2015; personal visit whereby I lost my lens cap in the bayou.

19. **Bayou Button**
    "What's Behind the Big Burp in Buffalo Bayou" by Marianella Orlando, *Houstonia*, April 28, 2016; "Press the red button to 'burp' Buffalo Bayou in downtown Houston" by Fox 26 Houston, May 6, 2016; "Secrets you probably didn't know about Houston" by Jessica Hamilton Young, *Houston Chronicle*, October 12, 2017; disappointing visit when the button wasn't working.

20. **Cajun Communion**
    https://www.treebeards.com/11460; http://www.christchurchcathedral.org/about-us/tours-history/; visited for red beans and rice, salvation.

21. **Houston Underground**
    https://www.downtownhouston.org/district/downtown-tunnels/; "Visiting the Downtown Houston Tunnels: What You Need to Know" by Katrina Madrinan, *Houston on the Cheap*, June 11, 2018; https://www.houstontx.gov/abouthouston/tunnelsystem.html; visited and ate tacos.

22. **Flight Times**
    http://www.1940airterminal.org/; *Houston Then & Now* by me; "Houston museums entertain, educate" by Ana Khan, *Houston Chronicle*, June 14, 2019.

23. **Boom Rooms**
Handbook of Texas Online, Carter Barcus, "San Jacinto Ordnance Depot," accessed July 14, 2019, http://www.tshaonline.org/handbook/online/articles/qbs04; ProPublica: "One of Texas' Most-Contaminated Former Military Installations Borders Houston Ship Channel" by Andrew Schneider, Houston Public Media, December 1, 2017; San Jacinto Old Depot, ProPublic "Bombs in Our Backyard" Series; "Where the Chemical Weapons Were Stored, Just Off Beltway 8," *Swamplot,* December 4, 2017.

24. **Irish Goodbye**
Houston Then & Now by me; Handbook of Texas Online, Stephen Fox, "Shamrock Hotel," accessed July 14, 2019, http://www.tshaonline.org/handbook/online/articles/ccs05; Handbook of Texas Online, Evan Kelly, "MCCARTHY, GLENN HERBERT," accessed July 14, 2019, http://www.tshaonline.org/handbook/online/articles/fmcaw; "Shamrock Hotel in Houston: Looking back at its luxurious opening" by Craig Hlavaty, *Houston Chronicle*, March 15, 2018; https://www.heritagesociety.org/the-shamrock-hotel-gone-but-not-forgotten; "The famous Shamrock Hotel's demolition began this week 30 years ago" by Craig Hlavaty, *Houston Chronicle*, May 31, 2017.

25. **Spring Training**
Houston Then & Now by me; U.S. National Register of Historic Places; "How Union Station became Astro's home" by Dave Ward, October 8, 2018, Dave Ward's Houston; "The History Of Minute Maid Park In 1 Minute" by Mire Milla, Culture Trip, June 2016; "Field Of Screams" by Leigh Montville, *Sports Illustrated,* May 22, 2000; personal visit.

26. **All Tapped Out**
Handbook of Texas Online, Lorelei Willett, "Gulf Brewing Company," accessed July 14, 2019, http://www.tshaonline.org/handbook/online/articles/dig02; Houston Ice & Brewing Co., *Houstorian Blog* (Tracey) December 27, 2006, https://houstorian.wordpress.com/2006/12/27/magnolia-ballroom/; *Lost Houston* by me; "Houston has a rich beer history" by Ronnie Crocker, *Houston Chronicle*, May 11, 2012; Harvey sucks.

27. **Oasis Out West**
http://clubwestside.com/; "Exotic animals at home at Westside Tennis Club," KPRC Houston, March 7, 2017; "Multimillion-dollar, 1,200-foot lazy river being installed in west Houston" by Darla Guillen, *Houston Chronicle*, December 30, 2016; "Westside's story: Club transforms from tennis to family-centered fitness resort" by Cynthia Lescalleet, *Houston Chronicle*, April 25, 2012.

28. **Lost and Found**
Lost Houston by me; "City Hall and Market House," *Houstorian* blog entry https://houstorian.wordpress.com/2006/12/18/city-hall-and-market-house/; https://www.downtownhouston.org/guidedetail/sights-attractions/old-city-hall-clock-plaza/; "Market Square clock gets a new identity—musically and visually" by Steven Brown, *Houston Chronicle*, September 25, 2013; "Houston's historic clock tower gets new life: Market Square Park to be awash in computer chimes" by Joel Luke, *CultureMap Houston*, September 27, 2013.

29. **What Fries Beneath**
https://www.bubbastexasburgershack.com/; delicious personal research; stopped by for delicious bison burger. Had bucket of Lone Star just to be thorough in research.

30. **Fantasy Island**
http://leilowhtx.com/; personally earned killer rum hangover; "Houston tiki bar losing its mugs to customers" by Craig Hlavaty, *Houston Chronicle*, July 2, 2014; fun Saturday afternoon drinks.

31. Act II, New Scene
Lost Houston by me; https://www.hermannpark.org/poi/125/; https://www.milleroutdoortheatre.com/past-and-present/; "Miller Outdoor Theatre: A Uniquely Houston Experience for 87 Years" by Debbie Z. Harrell, *Houston History Magazine*, Volume 7, Number 2, 2011; personal visit whereby I told two schoolgirls they'd be in the book and then you can't really see them in the shot (sorry, y'all).

32. Lock 'n' Love
"Love locks were a nuisance in Paris, but in Houston they're a sweet touch" by Maggie Gordon, *Houston Chronicle*, August 16, 2018; "Houstonians Are Attaching Their 'Love Locks' To Buffalo Bayou's Rosemont Bridge," *Swamplot,* June 9, 2015; "Houston's 8 Greatest Vantage Points for Those Dramatic Downtown Skyline Views" by Katharine Shilcutt, *Houstonia,* January 7, 2017; personal visit.

33. Domestic Beer
https://www.orangeshow.org/beer-can-house; "It took 20 years and 50,000 beer cans to finish this Houston home" by Brandi Smith, KHOU 11, January 24, 2019; "14 Best Things to Do in Houston," *Conde Nast Traveler*, October 11, 2018; place is great.

34. Concrete Jungle
https://www.cement.org/; https://www.hmdb.org/results.asp?SeriesID=312; https://www.tjp.us/blog/artist-albin-polasek-and-the-1932-time-capsule/; personal visit + tetanus shot.

35. Backwards Bar
Handbook of Texas Online, Marilyn M. Sibley, "NO-TSU-OH," accessed July 14, 2019, http://www.tshaonline.org/handbook/online/articles/lln01; "This is how Houston partied 100 years ago" by Craig Hlavaty, *Houston Chronicle*, September 7, 2016; http://notsuoh.com/; personal visit whereby I was afraid there would be slam poetry all of a sudden.

36. Seacret Passage
https://www.houstonmaritime.org/; "Houston Maritime Museum Sets Sail for Canal St." by Dan Singer, *Swamplot,* July 26, 2018; "Maritime Museum moving to the port it celebrates" by Sarah Scully, *Houston Chronicle*, March 14, 2016. https://www.atlasobscura.com/places/houston-maritime-museum; brief personal voyage.

37. Cheap Rounds Underground
http://valhalla.rice.edu/; "Bartender at Rice Institution Valhalla Threatens to Cut Off Alumnus's Necktie" by Brittanie Shey, *Houston Press,* November 18, 2013; "Valhalla is smart choice on Rice campus" by Marc Brubaker, *Houston Chronicle,* September 5, 2012; http://houston.culturemap.com/guide/bars/valhalla/

38. Room 322
"The story behind ZaZa's 'goth dungeon closet'" by Sarah Rufca, *Houston Chronicle*, February 20, 2103; "A Weird Hotel Room in Houston Is Freaking Reddit Out" by Tamlin Magee, *Vice*, February 26, 2013; "UPDATED: Does Hotel ZaZa Have a Creepy, Hidden Room They Don't Want You to Know About?" by Craig Malisow, *Houston Press,* February 18, 2013; "Floorplan for supposed sex-dungeon in Houston's Hotel ZaZa" by Cory Doctorow, *BoingBoing,* February 21, 2013.

39. Secret Specials
Taste of Texas personal correspondence; KPRC Click2Houston Food Friday: Bernie's Burger Bus Flamin' Hot Cheeto Mac & Cheese Burger; "This Week in Houston Food Events: Get Your Hands on a Flamin' Hot Cheetos Mac n Cheese Burger" by Brooke Viggiano, November 26, 2018; "The Secret Menu Items of Houston Restaurants" by Phaedra Cook, *Houston Press,* January 11, 2016; "Secret Menus for Austin Favorites" by Terri Gruca, KVUE ABC Austin, October 3, 2017; https://torchystacos.com/menu/secret-menu/

40. Game On
https://www.joystixgames.com/pacman-fever-friday/

41. Secrets of Old Texas
https://www.georgeranch.org/; "Experience Christmas at the George Ranch Historical Park" by Troy Schulze, Houston Public Media, December 20, 2018.

42. Underground Information
"Westland Bunker" by Jesse Mendoza, *Community Impact Newspaper*, May 20, 2015; "Bizarre bomb shelter becoming data center" by Jennifer Dawson, *Houston Business Journal,* May 8 2003; "Continental Airlines Finds a Safe Haven in a Texas Bunker" by Melanie Trottman, *Wall Street Journal*, October 2, 2006; "Underground surprise awaits visitors" by Howard Roden, *Houston Chronicle*, April 9, 2005; https://www.houstonbunker.com/

43. Bedazzled
https://www.orangeshow.org/about-smither-park; "A Beautiful, Wonderful Park for the Late Stephanie and John Smither" by Steve Jansen, *Houston Press,* September 28, 2016; "8 Best Parks in Houston" by Marcy de Luna, *Conde Nast Traveler*, October 5, 2018; "Using found art, nearly 300 people contributed to whimsical Smither Park" by Keri Blakinger, *Houston Chronicle,* October 6, 2016; visited and talked with artists.

44. The Tree Branches of Government
Personal inquiry with expert Louis Aulbach; "The Hanging Oaks of Houston" by John Nova Lomax, *Houston Press,* July 17, 2009; Buffalo Bayou: An Echo of Houston's Wilderness Beginnings (http://www.epperts.com/lfa/BB80.html); personal visit.

45. Slanted City
Personal inquiry with expert Louis Aulbach; Handbook of Texas Online, Joe B. Frantz, "BORDEN, GAIL, JR.," accessed July 14, 2019, http://www.tshaonline.org/handbook/online/articles/fbo24.

46. Whispers, Ribbits, and More
"Rice University's secret symbols, inside jokes and elaborate pranks" by Francisca Ortega, *Houston Chronicle*, August 16, 2018; "Unlocking Rice University's hidden symbols and messages" by Dave Ward, *Dave Ward's Houston*, October 29, 2018; "We (Urban) Dare You To Find Rice's Frog Wall" by Danny Lopez, *Houston Press,* November 24, 2009 (we also did the Urban Dare race the article talks about). Personal visit to campus where my mediocre intelligence was confirmed.

47. House of Scribes
https://inprinthouston.org/; Houston Public Media, Inprint Margarett Root Brown Reading Series; "In Print announces 2019-2020 season with Ta-Nehisi Coates, Colson Whitehead" by Andrew Dansby, *Houston Chronicle*, July 1, 2019; brief discussion with management; took a number of workshops.

48. Downtown's Capitol
Handbook of Texas Online, David G. McComb, "HOUSTON, TX," accessed July 14, 2019, http://www.tshaonline.org/handbook/online/articles/hdh03; "The history of Houston's Rice Hotel" by Craig Hlavaty, *Houston Chronicle*, May 17, 2018; https://easttexashistory.org/items/show/78; https://texasalmanac.com/topics/history/capitals-texas; https://www.livetherice.com/history/

49. Passage to India
https://www.baps.org/Global-Network/North-America/Houston.aspx; "Passport to India" by Molly O'Connor, ABC13, September 12, 2018; "Stroll the beautiful temple grounds of the BAPS Shri Swaminarayan Mandir in Stafford" by Cody Swann, *365 Things to Do in Houston*, January 7, 2019; personal visit to facility.

50. **Grave Memories**
http://historichouston1836.com/english-colonists-graves/; Unlikely Outpost of Empire, New York Times, December 15, 1987; "Burial mounds in Houston tell the tale of Huguenots in Texas" by J.K. Wagner, for the *Express-News,* February 7, 2015; http://boilerroomproject.blogspot.com/2010/04/why-we-are-pirates.html; "Houston Is Haunting" by Anthony Nguyen, *Houston Press,* September 27, 2010; "Old 1840 City Cemetery," *Historic Houston* (blog) http://historichouston1836.com/old-1840-city-cemetery/; http://www.houstontx.gov/histpres/archives/bom/jeff_davis.html; personal visit in heat of summer.

51. **Dismounted Downtime**
https://www.houstontx.gov/police/mounted/visitors.htm; "Take a tour of HPD's horse barn this Spring Break" by Shern-Min Chow, KHOU 11 News, March 12, 2019; "Giddy-up to the HPD Mounted Patrol Stables" by Jill Jarvis, *365 Things to Do in Houston*, November 6, 2014.

52. **The Wright Stuff**
"Frank Lloyd Wright Homes Take Longer to Sell, But the Right Buyer Will Pay a Premium" by Alanna Schubach, *Mansion Global*, July 12, 2019; "There's Not a Single 90-Degree Angle in This Frank Lloyd Wright Home for Sale" by Jordi Lippe-Mcgraw, *Architectural Digest*, June 19, 2019; "Updated Frank Lloyd Wright Usonian asks $2.9M in Texas" by Megan Barber, *Curbed,* June 5, 2019; "Frank Lloyd Wright Home Hits the Market in Houston" by Alex Temblador, *Architectural Digest*, May 17, 2019; http://wrightsociety.com/

53. **Battle for the Buckle**
"2019 Houston Livestock Show and Rodeo™ Gold Buckle Foodie Award Winners Named," https://www.rodeohouston.com/News/Article/ArtMID/494/ArticleID/2454/2019-Gold-Buckle-Foodie-Award-Winners; https://www.rodeohouston.com/Visit-the-Rodeo/Attractions-Activities/Shopping-Dining; "The very best (or worst) carnival food at the Houston rodeo" by Greg Morago, *Houston Chronicle*, February 28, 2019; "Houston Livestock Show and Rodeo Gold Buckle Foodie Awards announced" by Click2Houston.com staff, February 26, 2018; delicious research.

54. **Houston's Juiciest Secret**
https://www.orangeshow.org/; https://www.roadsideamerica.com/story/3341; https://www.atlasobscura.com/places/orange-show; "Orange Show came to fruition from one man's dream" by Mark Collette, *Houston Chronicle*, September 30, 2016; personal visit and got the grand tour, too.

55. **Lost Cause**
https://easttexashistory.org/items/show/139; "Expansive exhibit highlights Houston's quiet but vital role during Civil War" by Chris Gray, *Houston Chronicle*, July 11, 2018; https://houstoncivilwarprisoncompound.weebly.com/about.html; "Dumped and Forgotten Below the Milam Street Bridge": Houston in the Civil War, Heritage Society Museum, Houston by Linda Gorski, Houston Archeological Society.

56. **Work Your Magick**
https://www.magickcauldron.com/; "Where to Find a Little Mysticism in Montrose: The Magick Cauldron" by Emily Juhasz, *Houstonia*, January 31, 2017; "6 Great Places to Buy a Gift for Your Favorite Witch" by Chris Lane, *Houston Press*, October 20, 2015; https://www.youtube.com/watch?v=L3Cao1FIKoA; "The business of Magick" by Claudia Kolker, *Houston Chronicle*, October 31, 2016.

57. **Dark Waters**
"What lies beneath: 127 cars in the bayous" by Gabrielle Banks, *Houston Chronicle*, October 20, 2015; https://www.hcfcd.org/our-programs/submerged-vehicle-removal-project/; Cars, bodies sunken in Houston's bayous? by Derek Anderson, *USA Today*, May 14, 2014; "12 cars pulled out of Houston bayou in 6 days" by Cindy George, *Houston Chronicle*, February 2, 2106.

58. **Dome Sweet Home**
"Astrodome once featured Houston's gaudiest apartment" by Brian Reynolds, *Houston Chronicle*, September 22, 2017; "Inside Roy Hofheinz's Lavish Private Penthouse Suite" by Catherine D. Anspon, Paper City; "30 years ago: Hofheinz's Astrodome suite, Bush avoids a dog bite, UnNatural History at Sharpstown" by J. R. Gonzales, *Houston Chronicle*, March 30, 2018; "7 Floors Decorated in 'Early Farouk' : Hofheinz's Gaudy Suite in Astrodome Being Razed" by Michael Kennedy, *Los Angeles Times,* March 18, 1988.

59. **Bodies of Knowledge**
https://www.thehealthmuseum.org/; "Touch (Virtual) Bacteria in The Secret World Inside You at The Health Museum" by Jef Rouner, *Houston Press*, February 6, 2019; "New Health Museum exhibit in Houston lets you slip inside hyper-realistic skin suits," ABC13 (KTRK); "The Houston Health Museum is Now a Smithsonian Affiliate" by Allyson Waller, *Houstonia,* July 27, 2017; personal visit where I think I climbed in a colon.

60. **The Man Behind the Scan**
https://www.mdanderson.org/about-md-anderson/facts-history/who-was-md-anderson.html; https://www.mdanderson.org/about-md-anderson/facts-history.html; Handbook of Texas Online, Mary Jane Schier, "University of Texas M. D. Anderson Cancer Center," accessed July 14, 2019, http://www.tshaonline.org/handbook/online/articles/kcu26; https://www.tmc.edu/news/2015/05/the-history-and-legacy-of-the-m-d-anderson-foundation/; got cancer just to do this article (kidding), that was a coincidence, and I'm fine now.

61. **Free Parking**
http://jacksonstbbqhouston.com/wp-content/uploads/2015/08/Jackson-StreetBBQ_Parking.pdf; https://www.texasmonthly.com/bbq/jackson-street-bbq-2015/; "Smoked Out: Jackson Street BBQ" by Carlos Brandon, *Houston Press*, July 2, 2019; personal visit.

62. **Giants Among Men**
"Sculptor David Adickes updates Houston on the status of some of his very visible public art" by Craig Hlavaty, *Houston Chronicle*, March 21, 2018; "David Adickes Is Larger Than Life" by Roxanna Asgarian, *Houstonia,* December 29, 2017; "Meet the artist behind the Sam Houston statue: David Adickes" by Hannah Zedaker, *Community Impact Newspaper,* January 15, 2018; personal visit.

63. **Officers and Gentlemen**
Handbook of Texas Online, Bruce A. Olson, "Houston Light Guards," accessed July 15, 2019, http://www.tshaonline.org/handbook/online/articles/qjh02; https://www.youtube.com/watch?v=Nb7AMoOSLY0; "Old Houston Light Guard mixed marching, business and politics" by Betty T. Chapman, *Houston Business Journal*, November 19, 2009; http://www.texasmilitaryforcesmuseum.org/36division/archives/143/14301.htm; personal visit.

64. Survival of the Smartest
"Seventeen Years After the Enron Scandal, Jeff Skilling Returns" by Mimi Swartz, *Texas Monthly*, September 10, 2018; "See what happened to key players in Enron scandal" by Chronicle Staff, *Houston Chronicle*, July 9, 2019; "Former Enron CEO Jeff Skilling Released From Prison" by Chris Morris, *Fortune,* August 31, 2018; *Gaille Energy Blog*, Issue 19, Gaille Law; Enron Fast Facts, CNN Library, April 24, 2019; "Former Enron CEO Jeff Skilling out of prison, sent to halfway house" by L.M. Sixel, *Houston Chronicle*, July 9, 2019.

65. Tunnel Vision
https://www.hermannpark.org/poi/73/; "Houston's own It's A Small World ride: The Hermann Park train gets a new magical tunnel" by Joel Luks, *CultureMap Houston*, February 16, 2014; "Houston's Under-the-Radar Art Havens" by Annie Gallay, *Paper City,* April 19, 2018; https://www.jamescohan.com/artists/trenton-doyle-hancock; Trenton Doyle Hancock profile, Art21; "Review: Marvel Universe, this is not. A peek inside Trenton Doyle Hancock's Moundverse" by David Pagel, *Los Angeles Times,* January 22, 2019; personal visit.

66. Ghost Guns
Handbook of Texas Online, Jeffrey William Hunt, rev. by David Pomeroy and James V. Woodrick, "TWIN SISTERS," accessed July 15, 2019, http://www.tshaonline.org/handbook/online/articles/qvt01. "Hunt for the Twin Sisters Cannon" by C. David Pomeroy, *Early Texas History*, July 5, 2013; "Who were the famous Twin Sisters and what happened to them after the Battle of San Jacinto?" *Historic Houston* blog; "Twin Sisters" by Mike Cox, TexasEscapes.com, April 5, 2005; visit to park.

67. Trained Artists
"'Be Someone' artist speaks about famous statement," ABC 13 (KTRK) by Pooja Lodhia, May 28, 2016; "Q&A: Exclusive interview with Houston street artist 'Be someone'" by Leif Hayman, UHCL The Signal, May 1, 2017; "Meet the artists behind the 'Be Someone' light show" by Stephanie Whitfield, by KHOU.com, November 22, 2017; "'Be Someone' as an official Houston landmark? For now it will need to remain a folk icon... " by Craig Hlavaty, *Houston Chronicle*, January 4, 2018; "Is 'Be Someone' bridge graffiti or a landmark? Thousands sign petition" by KHOU.com, January 4, 2018.

68. Recreational Replay
"The 'A' Games – Ancient Games Tournament," ArcheologyNow, Archeological Institute of America, Houston Society; personal inquiry with event coordinators; "EXPERIENCE: Ancient Games Tournament Returns," Houston Archaeology Institute of America, January 21, 2018; "11 Ancient Board Games" by Mark Mancini, *Mental Floss*, March 1, 2016; "More than child's play, board game festival highlights historical significance" by Bridget Balch, *Houston Chronicle*, November 5, 2016.

69. Secret Sanctuary
https://houstonaudubon.org/sanctuaries/edith-moore/edith-moore.html; Edith L. Moore Nature Sanctuary Fact Sheet, Houston Audubon Society; personal visit; "Houston sanctuary is a bird paradise" by Gary Clark, *Houston Chronicle*, September 30, 2011.

70. **Surrounding Surnames**
Handbook of Texas Online, David G. McComb, "HOUSTON, TX," accessed July 15, 2019, http://www.tshaonline.org/handbook/online/articles/hdh03; Handbook of Texas Online, Lionel M. Schooler, "WESTHEIMER, MITCHELL LOUIS," accessed July 15, 2019, http://www.tshaonline.org/handbook/online/articles/fwets; Handbook of Texas Online, Julia Beazley, "HARRIS, JOHN RICHARDSON," accessed July 15, 2019, http://www.tshaonline.org/handbook/online/articles/fha85; Handbook of Texas Online, Amelia W. Williams, "ALLEN, AUGUSTUS CHAPMAN," accessed July 15, 2019, http://www.tshaonline.org/handbook/online/; Handbook of Texas Online, Amelia W. Williams, "ALLEN, JOHN KIRBY," accessed July 15, 2019, http://www.tshaonline.org/handbook/online/articles/fal21; Handbook of Texas Online, George T. Morgan, Jr., "KIRBY, JOHN HENRY," accessed July 15, 2019, http://www.tshaonline.org/handbook/online/articles/fki33

71. **Pipe Dreams**
"Big Oil Meets Folk Art at Eclectic Menagerie Park" by John Nova Lomax, *Texas Monthly,* October 20, 2017; https://www.atlasobscura.com/places/eclectic-menagerie-park; "Metal menagerie off Texas 288 springs from the mind of art-loving owner of Texas Pipe & Supply" by Chris Gray, *Houston Chronicle,* January 3, 2018; "What the Hell's on the Side of the Road?" by Michael Hardy, *Houstonia,* August 1, 2013; personal visit.

72. **Beaver Bubbles**
https://www.buc-ees.com/katycarwash.php; It's official! Buc-ee's car wash is now the longest in the world, ABC13 (KTRK), November 16, 2017; "This Buc-ee's in Katy Has the World's Longest, Trippiest Car Wash" by Sarah Rufca Nielsen, *Houstonia,* October 30, 2017; "Guinness says Buc-ee's carwash in Katy is world's longest" by Mike Glenn, *Houston Chronicle,* November 16, 2017; got truck washed.

73. **Underground Grub**
http://conservatoryhtx.com/; personal visit; "Conservatory, Houston's First Food Hall, Now Open in Downtown Houston" by Phaedra Cook, *Houston Press,* April 13, 2016; "What's in store at Conservatory, Houston's first food hall" by Greg Morago, *Houston Chronicle,* May 16, 2016; "Houston's Underground Dining Goes Upscale" by Jailyn Marcel, *Paper City*, July 8, 2016; macked down on pizza.

74. **Slam Dunk Sermons**
"This week in 1975 The Summit opened for concerts and basketball" by Craig Hlavaty, *Houston Chronicle,* November 14, 2017; "What Was Your Favorite Concert at The Summit?" by Chris Gray, *Houston Press,* November 7, 2012; "From feed store to basketball arena, Lakewood Church ministers to city of second chances" by Allan Turner, *Houston Chronicle,* September 7, 2016; https://www.lakewoodchurch.com/about/history; "10 years ago: Lakewood Church, Joel Osteen move into Houston's Compaq Center" by Craig Hlavaty, *Houston Chronicle,* July 14, 2015.

75. **Foreign Goods**
Yelp's The Best 10 International Grocery in Houston, TX; delicious personal visits; http://www.phoeniciafoods.com; http://www.viethoa.com/; https://www.visithoustontexas.com/things-to-do/shopping/specialty-markets/; https://www.hmart.com/; http://www.afghanhalalmarket.com/

76. **'80s Action**
https://www.imdb.com/title/tt0081696/locations; https://www.movie-locations.com/movies/t/Terms-Of-Endearment.php; "'Terms of Endearment' home hits the market" by Torrie Hardcastle, *Houston Chronicle*, February 19, 2014; https://www.brennanshouston.com/videos/brennans-houston-terms-endearment-history/; "10 Movies You Didn't Know Were Filmed in Houston" by Morgan at Culture Trip, January 2016; "Hollywood in Houston: Top 13 films made locally" by ABC13 (KTRK), March 4, 2018.

77. **Luv Ya Blues**
http://houstonbluessociety.org/index.html; https://www.thebigeasyblues.com/; "Houston Blues Museum Archives Find Home at Rice University" by Catherine Lu, Houston Public Media, July 11, 2019; "Celebrating the city's blues heritage" by Andrew Dansby, *Houston Chronicle*, February 22, 2012; "A little-known fact: Houston is the blues capital" by Rick Mitchell, *Houston Chronicle*, September 30, 2007; "The Rest of the Best: Houston's Top 8 Blues Clubs" by William Michael Smith, *Houston Press*, April 5, 2012; got blues just for this book.

78. **Fine Lines**
Handbook of Texas Online, Robert A. Rieder, "ELECTRIC INTERURBAN RAILWAYS," accessed July 15, 2019, http://www.tshaonline.org/handbook/online/articles/eqe12; *Houston Electric: The Street Railways of Houston, Texas,* by Steven M. Baron. (Read this book, it's amazing.)

79. **Dang, Y'all**
https://www.tvjohnny.net/; "This is what it's like waiting to meet Johnny Dang, Houston's King of Bling" by Wei-Huan Chen, *Houston Chronicle*, November 15, 2018; "From Beyoncé to Cardi B, celebrities rock grills and jewelry by Houston's Johnny Dang" by Marcy de Luna, *Houston Chronicle*, March 22, 2019; "Johnny Dang Partners With Warner Bros. for One-of-a-Kind 'Godzilla' Pendant," *HypeBeast,* May 2019; "Johnny Dang & Paul Wall Launch Largest Jewelry Shop Yet" by Brandon Caldwell, *Houston Press*, October 24, 2016.

80. **Newbie Translations**
"See what the Astroworld site looks like 50 years after the park opened" by Craig Hlavaty, *Houston Chronicle*, June 1, 2018; Handbook of Texas Online, Jill S. Seeber, "Hofheinz, Roy Mark," accessed July 15, 2019, http://www.tshaonline.org/handbook/online/articles/fho87; "LOL, People Really Think Beyoncé, a Queen Amongst Us, Broke Royal Protocol" by Starr Bowenbank, *Cosmopolitan,* July 15, 2019; https://www.houstonballet.org/about/nutcracker-market/; 'Pancho Claus' keeps tradition alive despite health scares, ABC13 (KTRK), November 23, 2018; "35 years later, UH's Phi Slama Jama teams still a hot topic" by Melanie Hauser, *Houston Chronicle*, March 28, 2019; "Sip on 'Slime in the Ice Machine' at this new Montrose patio bar" by ABC13 (KRTK) by Pooja Lodhia, June 26, 2019; "The 15 things I Googled when I moved to Houston" by Julian Gill, *Houston Chronicle*, August 10, 2018.

81. **The Butler Did It**
https://tshaonline.org/handbook/online/articles/fri03; "The Strange Case of the William Marsh Rice Murder" by Catherine Matusow, *Houstonia,* November 26, 2018; http://historichouston1836.com/rice-institute/; "William Marsh Rice's lawyer did him in to divert millions from college" by David Krajicek, *Daily News,* December 5, 2010; visit to campus.

82. **Say "Cheese"**
https://www.houstondairymaids.com/; "How Houston Dairymaids Stepped Up Houston's Cheese Game" by Gewndolyn Knapp, *Houstonia,* February 25, 2019; "10 Texas Cheeses Every Houstonian Should Try" by Gwendolyn Knapp, *Houston Press*, February 16, 2017.

83. **Storage Tours**
https://www.hmns.org/education/adults/offsite-collections-storage-tours/; "You Can Take A Secret Tour To See The Most Insane Hidden Museum Exhibits In Houston" by Kelly Martin, Narcity, May 3, 2019; "Peek inside the Houston Museum of Natural Science archives" by Craig Hlavaty, *Houston Chronicle*, May 29, 2018.

84. **Film al Fresco**
https://rooftopcinemaclub.com/houston/; went and saw *Jaws* and it was awesome; "Rooftop movie theater opens this week in Uptown Houston" by Michelle Homer, KHOU 11, October 1, 2018; "Houston's first rooftop cinema reveals prideful new summer lineup and fun themed nights" by Steven Devadanam, *CultureMap Houston*, May 1, 2019; "Rooftop Cinema Club opens in Houston" by Cary Darling, *Houston Chronicle*, October 4, 2018.

85. **Naked and Unafraid**
http://emeraldlakeresorthouston.com/; "Villager Q & A: Fred Everson, controller Emerald Lake nude resort" by Jeff Forward, *Houston Chronicle*, July 14, 2018; "Go Jump in the Nake" (respect for that title) by Catherine Matusow, *Houstonia*, July 8, 2015.

86. **Wing Stop**
https://www.hmns.org/cockrell-butterfly-center/; INSIDE ACCESS: Cockrell Butterfly Center, KHOU 11, September 20, 2018; "Houston nature centers and preserves to explore with kids," not attributed, *Houston Chronicle*, June 14, 2019; https://gov.texas.gov/film/trail/cockrell_butterfly_center; visited museum.

87. **Locally Sourced Welcome**
https://www.houstongreeters.org/; "Houston Jails & Prisons, Super Neighborhoods, & Houston Greeters: Houston Matters for Wed., Dec. 18, 2013" by Craig Cohen, December 18, 2013; "The 10 Best Ways to Entertain Yourself for Free Around Town" by Katharine Shilcutt, *Houstonia*, October 24, 2016.

88. **The Death and Diamonds Tour**
Personal correspondence with Vicki Clakley

89. **Garage-Mahal**
https://artcarmuseum.com/; brief personal visit; Check out the latest from Houston's art scene, *Houston Chronicle*, July 10, 2019; https://www.atlasobscura.com/places/artcar-museum

90. **Underground Comedy**
http://www.thesecretgrouptx.com/; hilarious personal visit; Are Your Puns the Most Groan-Worthy of All? By Chris Gray, *Houstonia*, July 20, 2018.

INDEX